The Key to Music's Genetics

The Key to Music's Genetics

Why Music is Part of Being Human

Christian Lehmann

THAMES RIVER PRESS

The Key to Music's Genetics

THAMES RIVER PRESS
An imprint of Wimbledon Publishing Company Limited (WPC)
Another imprint of WPC is Anthem Press (www.anthempress.com)
First published in the United Kingdom in 2014 by
THAMES RIVER PRESS
75–76 Blackfriars Road
London SE1 8HA

www.thamesriverpress.com

Original title: *Der genetische Notenschlüssel*
Author: Christian Lehmann
© 2010 F.A. Herbig Verlagsbuchhandlung GmbH, München
www.herbig.net
English translation © Holger Flock 2014
Edited by Matthew Grundy

All rights reserved. No part of this publication may be reproduced
in any form or by any means without written permission of the publisher.

The moral rights of the author have been asserted in accordance
with the Copyright, Designs and Patents Act 1988.

All the characters and events described in this novel are imaginary
and any similarity with real people or events is purely coincidental.

A CIP record for this book is available from the British Library.

ISBN 978-1-78308-028-1

This title is also available as an ebook.

The translation of this work was in part supported by a grant from the Goethe-Institut, which is funded by the Ministry of Foreign Affairs.

OXFORDSHIRE LIBRARY SERVICE	
3303035110	
Askews & Holts	01-Dec-2014
780.1	£16.95

For Therese, Victoria and Julius

CONTENTS

Prelude ix

I. Musical Nature *Lento* 1
   Music and Myth 1
   Animal Music 4
   Relative Pitch 11
   Clapping and Dancing: The Synchronous Movement 15
   The Human Voice 21
   The Evolutionary "Benefit" 24
   Lullaby in the Savannah 30
   Together We Are Strong 33
   Easier Sung than Said 39

II. Musical Culture – *Andante ma non troppo* 47
   Mammoths, Bone Flutes and Sheet Music 47
   Size and Number, Harmony and Character 52
   Singing for the Heavens 61
   Music on Earth 66
   The Invention of the Audience 69
   A Song in All Things 72
   Highlights of Modern Times 83

III.	Music and Person – *Espressivo*	89
	Goosebumps, Antibodies and Endorphins	89
	Music and Healing	97
	Does Mozart Make You Smart?	105
	Adorno and the Consequences	112
	Turning On and Turning Off	118
	Persona	123
IV.	Risk More Music – *Resonance*	127
	Conscious Listening	127
	For Each Child Ten Songs	131
	Good Paths	138
Notes		145
Bibliography		151
Acknowledgements		155

PRELUDE

On a mountainside on the right bank of the Ach, near the little town of Schelklingen in the Swabian Jura, towers a mighty boulder of Jurassic rock. It's no coincidence that this natural monument is called Hohle Fels (hollow boulder), because inside is one of the largest caves in southern Germany. A 95-foot tunnel leads to a spacious hall that opens up to an area of about 5,400 square feet.

Hohle Fels isn't only an impressive natural monument; like many other caves in the Swabian Alps, it has been visited and inhabited since the dawn of time. Researchers first began to show interest in the karst cave in the nineteenth century, and since the 1930s archaeologists have been methodically excavating there and in other caves in the Swabian Alps for relics of our ancestors from the Stone Age.

One September day in 2008, the eighteen-year-old Katharina Koll is going back to work with the so-called leaf and square, a fine masonry trowel. Kathrina is an apprentice in archeotechnics at the Hohe Fels excavation site, studying how to deal with modern surveying equipment. A few days ago, the excavation leader Maria Malina proposed that she join the team and actually dig by herself as recognition of her expertise and work. Normally, only students of archeology are offered this great opportunity.

Shortly before, the archaeological team from the University of Tübingen had made a spectacular find in Hohle Fels: several fragments of a female figure, approximately two and a half inches in height and carved from mammoth ivory, at least 5,000 years older than the famous Venus of Willendorf from the Vachau region in lower Austria, and thus the oldest known artistic representation of a person. Katharina, then, digs in a newly opened grid that borders the site of the Venus of Hohle Fels, hoping to find the other missing parts. The mild September sunlight doesn't penetrate the interior of the cave; the excavation must be carried out under artificial light. It's cold and the work is laborious and tedious. Katharina hasn't found much in the last few days: a few bones from the foot of a cave bear and pieces of coal, likely evidence of a charcoal grill in the Paleolithic Age.

Suddenly, a narrow, elongated piece of bone is unearthed. Katharina gently removes the surrounding soil with the trowel. The pencil-thin bone looks strikingly smooth. Katharina is excited. She recognizes instantly that this is no ordinary bone; it has been processed and polished by human hands. She exposes an approximately three-inch long fragment and takes it out of the ground. Now she sees that several round holes are cut into the bottom surface of the piece. Katharina immediately calls the excavation director. Maria Malina joins her, looks at the tube and says, "That looks like a flute!"

The spontaneous assessment seems to be confirmed. As early as the Paleolithic the flute looked very similar to the one we use nowadays. Over the next few days Twelve matching fragments of the small wind instrument, which was carved from a griffon vulture's bone, are recovered only twenty-seven inches away from the location of the Venus of Hohle Fels. Katharina Koll and her fellow archaeologists are overwhelmed with joy / ecstatic. They all know that it's a musical instrument in the Aurignacian cultural layer from the earliest days of modern *Homo sapiens* in Europe, some 35,000 to 40,000 years ago, and therefore a very special find. The excavation team get together in the evening and celebrate their success. One of the students brings a guitar along, and late into the night, music plays / echoes once again through the Ach valley.

What do you expect from a talent show? Probably less a sophisticated appreciation of art than a production that is exciting at best and nerve-racking at worst, and which doesn't really treat its musical gladiators sympathetically. That these stars are often intentionally "made" by the industry for a quick-fire career is a well-known critical point.

On the 9th of June 2007, the British broadcaster ITV airs the first episode of a new show in which singing talents aren't the only ones to introduce their skills and hope to get to the next round. The name of the show is *Britain's Got Talent*. That night, following a few more or less talented musicians, comedians and acrobats, a portly man in a cheap, dark gray suit from Woolworths enters the stage at the Wales Millennium Centre in Cardiff.

"Paul, why are you here today?" asks the beautiful woman in the jury in a tone of professional friendliness, the expression on her face conveying to the man that he had better answer with "Oh, I'm sorry, wrong room." But Paul says, "To sing opera." As he smiles with effort, one can see his crooked teeth. A few seconds of silence, and the members of the jury look at each other knowingly: Opera. That'll be the day. Next, the terse invitation: "Well then, begin."

While an orchestral prelude plays from a tape, Paul's tormented smile drops from his face. He pulls himself together and, focused, stares into the distance into the distance. Paul begins to sing "Nessun Dorma" from *Turandot* by Giacomo Puccini. The judge Simon Cowell, dreaded for his disparaging critiques, abruptly lifts his head in disbelief after the first three notes, stops chewing on his pencil and eyes the singer. The all-too-beautiful Amanda Holden swallows and breathes heavily. Her chest starts to quake – Paul Potts, the unassuming man who in real life sells cellular phones in the small Welsh town of Bridgend, can sing "classical music"; maybe not quite like Pavarotti, but still with an Italian flavor, with devotion, feeling, artistic sincerity and technical poise. Some women in the audience wipe tears from the corners of their eyes. At the crescendo towards the end of the aria, the "vincerò!" with the sustained high b (b4), the 2,000 spectators can no longer remain in their seats. The ending is overshadowed by the frenzied cheers of the audience. Amanda Holden is struggling to maintain composure, while Simon Cowell displays real, happy laughter (which he doesn't do often). Needless to say, Paul Potts won the competition. The video of Paul's appearance on *Britain's Got Talent* has had 115 million hits on YouTube at the time of publication. *German Telekom* has used his performance on *Britain's Got Talent* for a very successful commercial, resulting in the title catapulting once more into the German charts.

Mrs K. has probably not heard of Paul Potts. She lives in her own world. Mrs K. likes to go out occasionally, but she never makes it very far until she has to go back home. If you ask her where her home is she says: in Königsberg. Whether it's Monday or Friday Mrs K. cannot tell. In fact, she says little and rarely laughs. A nurse helps her when she gets dressed and eats. Her grandchildren visit her from time to time, but she no longer recognizes them. Mrs K. is ninety-two years old and lives in the dementia ward of a nursing home.

For several weeks now, the home has received an unusual visitor every Monday. His name is Michael and he comes to play music with a group of elderly residents. Michael is in his late thirties and is a professional music therapist. One day in June, he brings something special for Mrs K. He places a dark blue suitcase on the table and opens the lid. Mrs K., as so often, is sitting impassively in her chair. Suddenly, she sits up, awake and alert. She gets up slowly, walks over to the table and looks at the instrument for a while. With Michael's help she manages to turn the crank handle on the suitcase gramophone. Michael puts a shellac record on the velvet-covered turntable. Mrs K. carefully lifts the tone arm, the turntable starts to move and Mrs K. sets the tone arm on the shellac disc. The old lady listens and smiles. "Du hast Glück bei den Frau'n, Bel Ami!" plays from the gramophone. All of a sudden Mrs K. sings along, her voice a little halting, but clear:

> Bist nicht schön, doch charmant,
> bist nicht klug, doch sehr galant,
> bist kein Held,
> nur ein Mann, der gefällt.[1]

"Do you know that song?" Michael asks. "Yes, of course," says Mrs K., "from the dance hall!" As Michael packs up the portable gramophone and says goodbye, Mrs K. squeezes the young man's hand, looks at him firmly and says, "But come and visit me again!"

The old hit becomes the key song for Mrs K. Her grandchildren notice that their grandmother speaks clearer after the music lesson and remembers more things – even if only for a short time. At one point, Mrs K.'s sixty-eight-year-old daughter, who lives abroad, comes to visit. One day, by chance, she meets the music therapist and has a short conversation with him. Michael tells the woman about her mother's success with the gramophone and the song, "Bel Ami." Mrs K's daughter is at once visibly moved and tells him about her mother, who used to sing the song in the kitchen back in the day. "My mother says that when I was two or three years old, I was sitting on the stairs and started to sing along: 'You're lucky with the ladies, Bel Ami,' even though I didn't know what it meant. Well, my name is Wilhelmine and when I was little I thought the song had something to do with my name."

Mrs K. passed away last November. "Bel Ami" accompanied her to her death.

What do the discovery of a flute from the Stone Age, the triumph of the singing cell phone salesman and the old lady's sudden recollection of a song from her youth all have in common? An easy question to answer at first glance, of course, because all three stories are about music. But apart from this general and obvious commonality, are there any other, deeper connections between these key aspects that mark out such widely spread areas of the field? Music is part of our behavior and influences body and soul. However, this acoustic "medicine" isn't a drug of civilization, as shown by the flute from the Hohle Fels and other similarly ancient bone or mammoth ivory flutes found in the Swabian Alps, in the French Pyrenees and in Lower Austria. Humans played the flute long before they built houses or invented the wheel.

Nicholas Conard, a professor of prehistory at the University of Tübingen and scientific director of the excavations in the caves of the Swabian Alps, believes that the bone flutes from the Stone Age were "used in everyday life and not just at specific; such as in ritual events."[2] He deduces this based on the fact that some of the flutes and flute fragments were found in the midst of stone tool fragments and the ordinary waste of animal bones and plant material. So, it's therefore likely that the Stone Age Swabians played at the table or entertained the toolmaker at work with music.

We will encounter the key words "everyday life" again and again as a theme in the following chapters: it runs like a red thread through the history of music and its relevance to humans. It's a key to the locked rooms of Mrs K.'s memory and brings a little more joy to her life, accomplished without a visit to a great symphony concert by a philharmonic orchestra, but by an old hit that Mrs K. first heard as a teenager in a dance hall and then included in her repertoire of songs in her kitchen.

What was the reason for the fascination with Paul Potts? The frenetic enthusiasm and emotions that the Welshman unleashed in the talent show with "Nessun Dorma" would have been missing at an opera. "A passable tenor" the theater audience would say. From a professional, engaged in a performance, one expects that he knows his calling; after all, he has studied for it (though this doesn't "necessarily" mean anything). However, in Cardiff came this pleasant, unremarkable guy, out of a phone shop and onto the stage, and quickly exceeded all expectations – like Cinderella and Superman put together. We now know that Paul took, sporadically, private singing lessons and had already sung on stage in an amateur opera. Still: he is the guy next door. Just like other people play on the computer or go skiing in their spare time, Paul has always sung.

His popularity also touched another dimension. Many people who followed Paul's appearance or downloaded the video had never been to an opera or a classical concert. "Classical" singing is often perceived, by listeners who are used to what is commonly called "pop" or "modern" music, as artificial and a matter for the imaginary elite. The cell phone salesman from Bridgend proved otherwise. To sing like that suddenly doesn't seem so much like witchcraft, but something almost normal – as normal as Paul Potts.

Musical behavior and musical stimuli influence body and soul. They can trigger strong emotions, cause goosebumps, speed up the heartbeat and breath, and bring tears to the eyes – just like Paul Potts's performance did. Sometimes the effects of playing or listening to music can even surpass the reach of medication; for example, when a song revives a nearly extinct memory. Recent studies have shown that music therapy doesn't only open up blocked ways of communication, but can partially replace the painkillers and sedatives of severely ill patients in intensive care.[3] So, singing, playing an instrument and listening to music affects the brain and body functions. Furthermore, our brain seems to have a very specific skill that serves solely to produce and experience music. This becomes particularly clear for people who can no longer speak after a traumatic brain injury, but can still sing – or vice versa. These and other observations from clinical practice will be discussed later in more detail.

When behavior is coupled with strong emotions – if we experience feelings of pleasure associated with this behavior so that we are motivated by our own endogenous self-reward mechanisms to do or just experience something special – and if there are also signs of a specialized adaptation of this behavior in the brain, then it's suspected that this skill or ability is not a purely cultural achievement, but part of our biology. However, the enjoyment of the subject and the emotional involvement alone doesn't allow us to deduce, for example, why football causes such strong emotions and drives millions of people into the stadiums and in front of the television – though not many actively go on to the field with a ball. Football was invented in England in the nineteenth century and was previously unknown to *Homo sapiens*. However, it addresses a wide range of behaviors that are in our nature, concerning the joy (preferably non-life-threatening) of competition and the need to come together in groups. Nevertheless, we most likely don't have a football gene or a football module in the brain. Our species would have had to develop it within 150 years, which for mice is perhaps an evolutionarily significant period of time, but not for humans.

On the other hand, it has been proven that man has made music since Paleolithic times. The long time span seems to be further evidence of biological behavior adaptation. Nevertheless, the wheels of evolution grind very slowly. Changes to our genetic and phenotypic features by mutation, recombination and selection can only be seen after hundreds or thousands of generations. Actually, the skulls of the Aurignacian people who carved flutes and small ivory figures 35,000 years ago hardly differ anatomically to the skulls of today's humans. Our brains haven't become any larger since then. So, from an emotional human perspective, it's an unimaginable, distant past; however, phylogenetically speaking, it's quite recent. Thus a contradiction to the previous assertion: 35,000 years of playing the flute are just a few points on the evolutionary scale (or just a few beats in the song) in the many millions of years of history's incarnation. So, is music nothing more or less than a cultural performance?

In fact, it would be presumptuous to look for the evolutionary "origin of music" in the bone flute found in Hohle Fels. In the first place, we don't know how many, much older musical instruments are still in the ground waiting to be discovered or have long since decayed because the instrument-maker cut them out of wood or a reed. Decisive, however, is the following notion: a musical instrument is a tool. Direct physical contact historically precedes the use of tools. Before humans ate with spoon and fork, they used their fingers. Until a much earlier ancestor (who at that time had just begun to walk without hands) had had the idea to kill an animal with the throw of a stone, the usual hunting technique still prevailed, stalking to close proximity and killing the animal with bare hands.

The primary bodily instrument for producing musical sounds is the voice. Those who set out for the first time to carve flutes already had tones in their heads because they could sing notes. There is no reason to doubt that the anatomically modern Aurignacian humans, who were gifted with artistic imagination, could use their voice as well as we can today. Anthropologists agree that even archaic *Homo sapiens* that lived almost 200,000 years ago in Africa would have had a respiratory system and vocal almost identical to those of modern humans.[4]

So, if we make an educated guess, we can say that singing, a primary form of musical expression, is evolutionarily at least twice as old as the oldest musical instruments found so far (if not much older).

Incidentally, this is also true for another primary musical expression: the rhythmic beating and clapping of hands.

The evidence that music is part of human nature amasses. Now there are only two more criteria missing for human ethology (the science of human behavior evolution), according to which the most important evidence for behavior lies in a strong genetically inherited foundation. One criterion is the question of the so-called anthropological universals. This refers to behavioral characteristics that can be observed to be similar in different cultures (before modern globalization). Details of social behavior are part of it; for example, the so-called eye greeting (a silent "hello" through brief eye contact, lifting of the eyebrows and a nod) or the incest taboo.

We will assess in more detail after the first section of this book. Just to what extent music can be understood as a "world language" anywhere on earth and how musical expression is similar or different in various traditions. However, there is also an agreement among anthropologists that all cultures of the world know something that sounds to Europeans like "music."[5] One has to formulate it somewhat indirectly because the European concept of music isn't always congruent with related concepts from other cultures.

To find elements of the *conditio humana*, the nature of humans, that exist independently of cultural teachings, behavioral scientists not only seek global "transcultural" comparisons, but also look in the nursery (which is the second important criterion). An ability that a baby displays before nurturing and socialization must either be genetically inherited or acquired *in utero*. The latter is unlikely in most cases, but it's discussed again and again in relation to music: do children have a knack for music because they hear their mother's voice *in utero* or can listen to her CDs through the abdominal wall? This question (and, incidentally, the likelihood of confusion between the already unpopular concepts of "innate" and "inherited") will occupy us again in both Chapters I and III. In any case, babies that are already a few months old are (as numerous studies have proven) receptive to music and apparently seem to prefer harmonious sounds to dissonant ones.[6]

As a first conclusion we note that if we listen to or play music, biological processes occur. A number of indications suggest that our ability to order sounds, and understand and appreciate them, isn't only "culture," but also "nature." Regardless, this statement hardly answers the question of the nature of the musical phenomenon. On the contrary, it leaves us with further questions: if music is a biological inheritance, can we find parts of that heritage back in the animal kingdom – in songbirds, for example? And is there any musical talent in our closest relatives, the great apes?

And also, what are the special capabilities of the mind and body that actually make up what is called "musical talent"? Furthermore: if music is in the genes, how did it get there? Did a sense of melody and rhythm provide a survival or reproductive advantage to those ancestors who possessed it? If so, in what way – and is this important for us modern people?

These questions will occupy us in the next chapter. We will collect evidence and statements about the "nature of music" in humans and animals from different scientific branches, take a closer look now and then and examine them critically, and link them together in order to assemble a clear and vivid picture. In Chapter II, we will embark on a journey through the musical cultural history of Europe and make quite a few stops to observe which role the ability of *Homo musicus* played in our cultural area over the centuries and what importance they assigned to music in their society. In Chapter III, we will switch our focus from society to the individual – in particular, how music affects the individual. Finally, in Chapter IV, we will take critical stock of how man has dealt and deals with music and musical talent, and point out perspectives for the future of this relationship.

I. Musical Nature

Lento

Music and Myth

A nymph of late there was
Whose heav'nly form her fellows did surpass.
The pride and joy of fair Arcadia's plains,
Belov'd by deities, ador'd by swains:
Syrinx her name, by Sylvans oft pursu'd,
As oft she did the lustful Gods delude:
(...)
Descending from Lycaeus, Pan admires
The matchless nymph, and burns with new desires.
A crown of pine upon his head he wore;
And thus began her pity to implore.
But e'er he thus began, she took her flight
So swift, she was already out of sight.
Nor stay'd to hear the courtship of the God;
But bent her course to Ladon's gentle flood:
There by the river stopt, and tir'd before;
Relief from water nymphs her pray'rs implore.

Now while the lustful God, with speedy pace,
Just thought to strain her in a strict embrace,
He fill'd his arms with reeds, new rising on the place.
And while he sighs, his ill success to find,
The tender canes were shaken by the wind;
And breath'd a mournful air, unheard before;
That much surprizing Pan, yet pleas'd him more.
Admiring this new musick, Thou, he said,
Who canst not be the partner of my bed,
At least shall be the confort of my mind:
And often, often to my lips be joyn'd.
He form'd the reeds, proportion'd as they are,

> Unequal in their length, and wax'd with care,
> They still retain the name of his ungrateful fair.[1]

The myth is the oldest method used by men to explain phenomena of which they couldn't rationally or historically justify the origin. In many traditions, musical instruments are given a mythical, divine origin. The story of Pan and the nymph Syrinx, who turns into a musical reed and gives the shepherd's flute its name (we also know it as a pan flute), found its way into Ovid's *Metamorphoses*. Ancient Greece also has a myth regarding the origin of the lyre, the most important musical instrument of the ancient world. It is the work of the newly born god Hermes: he kills a turtle, guts it, stretches cowhide over a shell, attaches goat horns as arms and affixes seven strings made of sheep intestines. Later he leaves the instrument with his brother Apollo as compensation for a quarrel. However, Apollo turns over the stringed instrument to Orpheus, who with his singing charmed animals, trees and even rocks.

This chapter concerns evolution, the scientific approach to the phenomenon of music – why, then, do we address myth at all at this point?

If we analyze myths not only as poetry, but as anthropologically meaningful and rewarding, as a manifestation of a collective unconscious, then two motives stand out: in the story of Syrinx and Pan (and elsewhere), the musical instrument and sound have an erotic significance; the episode of Hermes and the lyre concerns animals from a pastoral and farming culture (and the symbolically long-living, virtually immortal turtle), from whose bodies the instrument is created. Thus myth links music with life's necessities. In other words, it links the musical instrument as a symbol of music with life's essentials. But why have people been given the ability to sing? It seems that there exists no explanation.

In modern times, Jean-Jacques Rousseau was one of the first philosopher to discuss the origin of music.[2] He maintained that music and language have a common origin. In Rousseau's conception, prehistoric humans used their voice to sing, and communicated in *chansons* (songs) because *musique* (music) and *langue* (language) were, in their original state, one and the same. Only later did sound and the spoken word become independent, which Rousseau judged as an ominous development.

The idea that spoken language emerged from song has been popular for a long time. Heinrich Heine wrote in 1822 from Berlin

> What do you *sing* in Berlin that you know now, and I pose the question: what is *spoken* in Berlin? I deliberately talk about singing first because I am convinced that people sung before they learned to speak, as the metrical language preceded prose. In fact, I think that Adam and Eve offered melting adagios, declarations of love and scolded each other in recitatives. Did Adam also beat the time to the latter? Probably. This hitting a beat stayed with our Berlin populace through tradition, although singing fell into disuse. Our ancient parents chirped like canaries in the valleys of Kashmir. We have educated ourselves! Will birds also be able to talk? Dogs and pigs are on track; their barking and grunting is a transition from singing to proper speech.[3]

Also, Charles Darwin, founder of the theory of evolution, observed almost fifty years later, much like the German poet: "It appears probable that the progenitors of man, either the males or the females or both sexes, before acquiring the power of expressing their mutual love in articulate language, endeavoured to charm each other with musical notes and rhythm."[4] For this naturalist, however, it isn't about poetically glorifying or caricaturing a suspected primitive state. He writes these lines in his 1871 book *The Descent of Man and Selection in Relation to Sex*, his second major scientific work after *On the Origin of Species* (1859). In it, Darwin outlines his theory of the origin of man from animal predecessors, especially the relationship between man and ape. These revolutionary theses had already been made public at that time by two other scholars, the Englishman Thomas Henry Huxley and the German Ernst Haeckel, and quickly became a hotly debated topic.

Moreover, Darwin explains an essential principle of the theory of evolution. Besides *natural selection* (selection based on environmental conditions), there is another mechanism that affects the origin of species, namely *sexual selection*: selection based on the choice of a mate. Those who attract the opposite sex with certain physical or behavioral characteristics will have more progeny. Their offspring will inherit the attractive characteristics, which will manifest themselves over the course of evolution as a feature. Thus, for example, male peacocks have excessively long tail feathers that are impractical for movement; but can be turned into a magnificent wheel that peahens find attractive. Even the ability of many animal species (especially males) to produce complex melodic sounds led Darwin back to this mechanism of sexual selection. The sounds the male emits can be heard mainly during mating season and are obviously attractive to the opposite sex.

Animal Music

Since man, according to Darwin's view (and as it is generally accepted today), evolved from the pedigree of the animal kingdom, it is only natural to relate the behavior of humans to that of our animal relatives. Darwin arrived at his hypothesis about the original purpose of music as a means of courtship not only by a biological relationship between animals and humans, but also by deriving a relationship in communication between animal and human. Therefore, the fact that many sounds from the animal kingdom are "musical" to our ears because they are made up of harmonic waves, seems not to be a coincidence.

The theory of evolution is nowadays not only accepted in the world of scientific experts / science, but also in general by Western society and is widely regarded as a plausible model to explain the diversity of organisms, their relationships to each other and their role in the environment. Even most of the leading theologians of the Catholic and Protestant churches see no contradiction between scientific knowledge and Christian creationism.[5] They share the view that man – as the "crown of creation" – is in a biological, ancestral community with animals.

The first question of the evolutionary "origins" of our behaviors and mental abilities must therefore be: what qualities do we humans have in common with other species and how far back can we trace a characteristic in the family tree of vertebrates (or even all organisms)? In fact, the molecular genetic findings of kinship are striking: we share at least 95 percent, if not 99 percent, of our genetic material with chimpanzees; at least 78.5 percent with mice and we even have 60 percent of our DNA in common with the *Drosophila* fruit fly. For all obvious differences, at least among vertebrates, a high degree of similarity between comparable physiological processes that have a genetic basis should be expected. So, before tracking the "nature of music," we must first look for "music in nature." The virtuoso role in the animal concert is played by the inhabitants of the air – the terms "birdsong" and "songbirds" show how naturally we humans attribute musicality to blackbirds, thrushes, finches and starlings. Also, for the 4,000 "singing-capable" species of passerines, the name "songbirds" or Oscines has been established in zoological taxonomy (from Latin *canere* – "singing"). The feathered singers have played an important role in poetry and songs for centuries. The topos of birdsongs seems to be as important for poetic representations of love, longing and the *locus amoenus* (the pleasant place) as much as the brook or the moon. In particular, there are two types of birds that are praised and sung about again and again. Firstly, the nightingale, whose sweet, plaintive tones move the feelings of people in the early hours:

Alles schweiget, Nachtigallen
Locken mit süßen Melodien
Tränen ins Auge, Schwermut ins Herz.[6]

Secondly, the lark, because it soars into the sky and, as is said, sings the praises of God: "Laudat alauda Deum dum sese tollit in altum."[7]

Composers from different eras have been inspired by the sounds of the birds and written works in which wind instruments, string instruments or the human voice mimic the singing of birds. The Dutchman Jacob van Eyck (1590–1657), blind since birth, composed a series of variations for solo soprano flute named "The English Nightingale." At the beginning of the "Spring" concerto from Antonio Vivaldi's (1678–1741) famous *The Four Seasons* three violins artfully and convincingly represent the twittering of a bird trio. "Spring has come and is festively welcomed by cheerful singing birds," are the opening lines of the explanatory sonnet that the Venetian added to his composition.

Almost two hundred years later, Gustav Mahler (1860–1911) explained the musical imagery in the first line of his Symphony no. 1 with a programmatic title: "The introduction describes the awakening of nature in the earliest morning." Mahler removed this clarification later because the listener is able to grasp the scene without words and recognize the finch's song and the call of the cuckoo in the woodwinds.

Ralph Vaughan Williams (1872–1958), in *The Lark Ascending*, gave the solo violin the part of a singing skylark rising into the sky. In the twentieth century, the French composer Olivier Messiaen (1908–92) engaged intensively in birdsongs. "Just like Bartók roamed through Hungary in order to collect folk songs, I have roamed for many years the provinces of France in order to record the songs of birds," Messiaen said. He developed his compositions from these recordings. The Frenchman admitted, "In spite of my deep admiration for folk songs of the world, I do not think that one can find in human music, be it oh so inspiring, any melodies and rhythms that have the sovereign freedom of a birdsong."[8]

These are just a few examples of the artistic topos of the close relationship between people and birdsong. It touches us, but we cannot understand its meaning – except by magic! Richard Wagner (1813–83) explores this in *Siegfried*, when his hero listens to the singing of a forest bird and wishes he knew what it wants to tell him. After Siegfried kills the lindworm Fafner and gets a little dragon's blood on his tongue, he immediately understands the singing of the forest birds, which no longer sing with the sounds of a flute, but with a human soprano voice, pointing him in the right direction.

But what does science say? How do birds sing, what do they sing about and why do they do it? Like all vertebrates, birds have a voice box (larynx) at the upper end of their windpipe (trachea). This lacks, however, the vocal cords found in the mammalian larynx. Birds emit their sounds with another organ, the syrinx (like the nymph who was transformed into a reed), located in the two main bronchi branches at the bifurcation of the trachea. The air flowing out of the lungs makes the syrinx membranes oscillate and the intensity is altered by a complex muscular system. Usually the syrinx is surrounded by an air sac that acts as an additional resonating body.

The vocal tone production in the bird's syrinx functions similarly to that of the larynx in mammals; however, the organs are different. Therefore, voices of birds and mammals are not *homologous*. Homologous features come phylogenetically from the same root: the wing of a bird is homologous to the front leg of a crocodile and the arm of a human. If, however, organs of different origins have similar functions over the course of evolution and are therefore often also similar in appearance, then we talk about *analogy*. The forepaws of the mole and the forelimbs of a mole cricket are *analogous* to each other, just as it is with the syrinx of birds and the larynx of mammals.

The ability to produce complex melodies is innate to songbirds. But this doesn't mean that the songs are innate programs that run automatically. A wren knows about five to ten "songs." Each song consists of phrases that the bird has in his repertoire, but the order and arrangement of these musical elements are different in each song.

The songs of a male wren differ from each other and also from those of other wrens. Ornithologists have found that the repertoire of an older, experienced male is larger than that of a younger bird. The young bird learns to sing by listening to the songs of the adult wrens, divides them into segments and then reconnects these blocks into new original songs.[9]

But birds don't only learn from their conspecifics. Many songbirds are also able to absorb alien sounds from their environment and add them to their own repertoire. Many a suburban resident will have met a blackbird in their garden that can parody the sound of a bicycle bell deceptively well. Parrots (not belonging to the group of singing birds) are known to mimic highly differentiated human speech sounds, as corvids (which are among songbirds, but cannot sing) are also known to do.

The melodies of songbirds often exhibit rhythmic patterns, pitch conditions and tone combinations that are similar to those of human compositions. Therefore, some birdsongs address our musical perception.[10] American ornithologist Luis Baptista played a recording of a sequence of notes before his audience at a conference, and every listener – despite the change in pitch – immediately identified it as the opening motif of the Fifth Symphony by Ludwig van Beethoven: "Ba-ba-ba bamm." But in this case it was the call of the songbird *Henicorhina leucosticta*, a distant Mexican relative of the wren, rather than the Viennese classic.

As already mentioned, birdsongs often consist of short motifs that the feathered singer repeats many times, varying them and combining them with other motifs. These are precisely the principles on which human music is also constructed. Unlike in spoken language, in music we accept and appreciate persistent vocal repetitions as a means of creation and expression. We encounter the opening motif of the first movement of Beethoven's Fifth ("Ba-ba-ba bamm") in the course of this movement a hundred times over, literally or in a modified form. No less explicitly does Handel present it in his famous "Hallelujah" chorus. Both pieces have become international hits, like the songs "Waterloo" or "Money Money Money" by the pop group ABBA, in which the title motif is repeated many times.

In ancient times it was believed that birds sang for the joy of existence or even that they did it to amuse people and praise God. Natural scientists are not completely satisfied with this kind of reasoning. Ornithologists note that birds – and almost always only males – sing to defend their territory and for courtship.

How do ornithologists know this? They have established this from observing animals in the wild and from biological behavioral experiments. Male birds sing almost exclusively during the mating and nesting season. During this season the animals fight over their territory and often carry out vocal duels: the neighbor responds to the leader in staccato, so to speak, by taking his motifs and attempting to produce them with even more virtuosity. The songs of most birds fade away at the end of the breeding season.

A now-famous experiment demonstrates that birdsong actually meets the presumed function of defense against rivals. In the experiment, a great tit male is removed from his territory. Usually it doesn't take long for another tit to move into the vacated area. However, if the scientists place a speaker that emits the voice of a great tit in the bird's territory, then it remains unoccupied for longer: fellow tits are deceived by the fake voice and respect the acoustic signal of "I live here."[11]

The above-mentioned parodistic talent of some birds is obviously well-received by the opposite sex. The males of the satin bowerbird that can sing the most songs of other birds have the greatest mating success. Vocal repertoire seems to play an even greater role than the beauty of the decorated nest, with which the male satin bowerbird impresses his female.[12]

An interesting correlation can be observed between the "musical talent" and territorial behavior of these birds. Singers of elaborate and complex songs, such as the nightingale, defend their territories vigorously, while the musically simpler house sparrow treats its conspecifics in a sociable and friendly manner.

Notation of the singing of a song thrush.[13]

Is the key to the evolutionary understanding of the phenomenon of music in the behavior of songbirds? Striking parallelisms exist between birdsong and human music: the tones are generated in a similar way (albeit in another organ); the design principle of the songs is similar and their variety is based on ingenuity, flexibility and the ability to learn new things. So, do we share a musical heritage with birds? When we look at the family tree of vertebrates, it is clear that the branch from which both reptiles and birds emerged split off from the mammalian branch about 200 million years ago. Consequently, signs of any common musical heritage between birds and people should also be found among our closest mammals relatives.

In fact, the musical abilities of one large mammal have only become known in recent decades, as they were previously not accessible to our ears. Until the 1960s, marine scientists were not able to identify the strange, deep sounds, recorded in the oceans with an underwater microphone. Roger and Katherine Payne have been investigating the up-to-fifty-foot-long humpback whales (*Megaptera novaeangliae*) for decades and have demonstrated that these marine mammals emit complex, musically structured "songs". Humpback whales inhabit all oceans between the polar waters where they feed and the tropical seas where they mate and give birth, and travel many thousands of miles per year. The males sing during mating and their songs depict a distinct hierarchical structure: from individual sounds to "phrases," which in turn form "themes" by repetition and combination, which are then combined into a "song." These songs can be ultimately connected and create hours of song cycles.

Surprisingly, songs of humpback whales differ geographically. Whales in the territory of Hawaii sing a different "dialect" than whales from Australia or Europe. On the other hand, songs change rapidly, even though all males from one population sing roughly the same songs. Obviously, humpback whales change their repertoire "creatively" and pass it on to their own kind: a rare case of cultural transference in the animal kingdom.

However, if we look around the more familiar land mammals, it is difficult to find a species that would qualify for the title of "musical". Even after thousands of years domesticated ungulates like horses, cattle, sheep and goats are not able to produce complex, melodically and rhythmically structured vocalizations or to learn foreign sounds, nor does the obviously intelligent and trainable form of the wolf, the domesticated dog.

The assumption itself suggests that our nearest relatives among mammals, the primate, should have rudimentary, primitive musicality. Apes share a number of "progressive" features with humans: they can move around on two legs, have opposable thumbs, use tools, show emotions, display facial expressions, and have strong social tendencies that are intimately familiar. Accordingly, their cerebral cortex is strongly formed.

Indeed, there are species among the primates that give surprisingly melodic and rhythmically structured calls. The gibbon family (*Hylobatidae*) inhabits the forests of Southeast Asia and is closely related to the great apes. In the early morning hours the males and females often emit long-lasting songs; some species also sing in duet. However, there is one key feature that humans, birds and whales have in common that is missing from the gibbons: the ability for vocal imitation, for *vocal learning*. Gibbons sing genetically programmed patterns. They vary very little, don't compose and don't learn new things. At least that is the current state of our knowledge about these distant cousins.

Can one then call gibbons "musical" at all? American evolutionary biologist Tecumseh Fitch notes that the ability of *vocal learning*, to mimic with a voice, is the decisive condition of what we mean by musicality.[11] Crickets, toads and gibbons indeed possess vocal organs that can produce harmonious sounds, but they cannot use them "creatively." That is the main difference between their singing and those of birds, humpback whales and humans. The somewhat musical sounds of the Southeast Asian tree-dwellers are therefore not a model for a precursor of musical expression in humans.

Also sobering is the observation that the apes that are most closely related to us, such as African chimpanzees and bonobos, don't show even a smidgen of musical talent and are unable to imitate speech sounds. Two famous apes, the chimpanzee Washoe and the bonobo Kanzi, learned in captivity how to communicate with humans through sign language. However, they could never reproduce the language with their voice. Even though apes can think symbolically, they lack the ability of vocal learning.

What information leads us to the evolutionary biological view of "music-like" behavior in the animal kingdom? Numerous species produce specific rhythmically and melodically arranged sequences of tones that sound "musical" to human ears. Some of these animals also have the ability of vocal learning, meaning that they can mimic sounds and integrate them into their repertoire. This characteristic in humans is the very first condition of their musical behavior; neither playing the piano nor the melody of any song is innate to us, while the talent to learn these things is. The mere reproduction of an inherited, nonvariable, nonexpandable sound program is, however, not yet music. Music is only created through invention and expressiveness.

There is no connection between the ability for vocal learning and the relationships between the relevant animal groups in the family tree of vertebrates. Vocal learning has evolved independently in different families of birds and mammals as a behavioral adaptation. The structural similarities show that the evolution of very different organisms can under certain environmental conditions result in somewhat similar abilities, as in the phenomenon of analogy or *convergence*. However, analogy does not establish common musical roots in the vertebrate lineage. Ironically, our nearest relatives in the tree, the great apes, lack the ability for vocal learning. They don't even possess – as do gibbons – a "beautiful voice" with which to produce harmonic sounds. What makes the humans, the latest "model" of primates, musical can only come from our ancestry after the lineage of chimpanzees and humans split about 6 million years ago.

Therefore, the journey through the musical life in the animal kingdom doesn't bring us any closer to answering the question of what music means to the nature of man. To explore this question one has to look where the music plays: in humans. What are the skills that make us musical and that we look for in vain in our animal cousins?

Relative Pitch

Most Germans probably know the song "Der Mond ist aufgegangen" (The Moon has Arisen). If we take a survey in a pedestrian area and ask passersby to sing the first notes of this song, we would find a few brave volunteers that are willing to sing the familiar tune. We can denote its beginning without musical notation and regardless of the tone key by simply numbering the steps of a major scale and replacing the tones of the song with the corresponding figures:

1–2–1–4–3–2(long)–1
(Der Mond ist auf–ge–gan–gen)

If we record the "auditions" and listen to the vocal contributions of the interviewees consecutively, we will find that some people have sung the song higher, some lower. Men usually sing with a deeper voice than women, that's a given; but there are also higher and lower pitches among the women and men where even people with similar vocal characteristics reproduce the same song in different pitches when it's sung from memory and not accompanied by a musical instrument. Nevertheless, we would identify the melody of "Der Mond ist aufgegangen" (assuming the singer isn't completely tone deaf or thinking of a different song).

A similar experiment could be performed with orchestra musicians by asking them to play the first notes of a song by memory on their instruments. A violinist might do it in G major because this key is suitable for the violin, a pianist or organist would choose for simplicity C major (which only requires white keys) and a trumpet player would probably play the song in F major if he has an F-tuned trumpet handy. Even without the text we would recognize a well-known song, no matter what key it is played in or on what instrument. This statement isn't as trivial as it might seem. There are areas of perception where we remember (more or less accurately) absolute values. The size of a ten Euro note is relatively well memorized. A bill the size of a credit card would stand out for us just as much as one the size of the size of a chocolate bar. No doubt they would not be real. Our visual sense is quite reliable especially when determining colors (i.e. light wavelengths). A blue tomato would look odd to us even without a red one to compare it to, so that we would prefer not to eat it.

The difference between two colors (that is, the distance between two locations within the visible spectrum or a relation of two wavelengths), however, is not a relation that we could estimate and transfer. Therefore, the statement that "the yellow of apple A is closer to the green of apple B than to the red of apple C" is, according to humans, only approximate and subjective.

However, our perception of music works differently: we usually don't memorize the absolute pitch, but the distances between the notes (the so-called intervals).[15] They determine the contour of a melody. The step from "Der" to "Mond" in the popular song is clearly smaller than the jump from "ist" to "auf": the first interval is a whole tone step (also called a major second, the distance from the first to the second step on the musical scale), the second is a fourth (the distance from the first to the fourth step). That won't change even if the whole song is moved to a different pitch (e.g., moved up or down). If one sings or plays, instead of the 1–2–1–4 sequence, a sequence of 1–3–2–5, then we won't identify this tune with the beginning of "Der Mond ist aufgegangen." Our hearing is very acute and differentiates exactly to the fraction of a half step, yet it is also willing to generously adjust slightly out of tune intervals.

At this point we won't get away without a look at acoustics. From a physical viewpoint, the distances between musical scale steps are nothing but speed ratios of vibrations. A rapidly vibrating string sounds higher than a slowly vibrating string. The vibration speed is designated as a frequency (cycles per second). The frequencies of two tones at intervals of a fourth act as 4:3, the frequencies of a fifth as 3:2 and that of an octave as 2:1.

A musical "tone," in a purely physical sense, isn't a tone but a "sound." A "tone" in the physical sense only consists of a single vibration. (Those "pure tones" we know from a hearing test, for example, can only be approximately generated electronically.) A mechanical musical instrument and the human voice produce sounds that are composed of several partial tones, a key tone and more resonating overtones. The typical harmonics of a musical instrument are created by the spectrum of the overtones that the instrument generates. The harmonic spectrum of a flute is different from that of a violin, which means the ear is able to easily identify the different instruments by their sound.

The vibrations generated by the key tone and overtones are perceived by us as one unit. When the sound waves enter our ears they change the pressure in the fluid-filled cochlea of the inner ear and cause the tiny hair cells there to move, just like seaweed is moved by ocean waves. High frequencies bend hair cells at the beginning of the cochlea; lower frequencies reach cells in the center of the cochlea. Each deflected hair cell sends out a nerve impulse that is directed further to the auditory nerve, which in turn sends it to the brain.

If each "tone" already consists of many frequencies, not to mention a chord or even a group's successive sounds, one can imagine each musical event as a complex fireworks display caused by many individual impulses. The brain must now analyze these impulses and organize the information. Here, something astonishing happens: our brain only distills what's important out of the stimulus thunderstorm. When "Der Mond ist aufgegangen" is played in F major by a clarinet and listened to on one's auditory pathway, which of the frequencies can be regarded as "pitch" and which belong to "tone"?

From a comparison with known patterns, the timbre analysis results in "clarinet" or perhaps "wind instrument", depending on the experience of the listener. A deeper analysis, such as "the first tone is an F," however, remains missing in the brain of a "normal" listener because it doesn't store absolute frequency values in long-term memory. It does this quickly in the "working memory" in order to relate it to frequencies of preceding and subsequent tones. This creates "musically important" information that can be compared to the stored patterns in the long-term memory, which recognizes "1–2–1–4–3–2–1." At this point I know – that's "Der Mond ist aufgegangen."

In summary: in contrast to the more or less exact memory of the red color value of a tomato, most people don't remember any absolute pitches, but the relation of the pitches to each other. This ability is therefore called *relative pitch* (as opposed to *perfect pitch*). Relative hearing is of central importance to processing music because through this cognitive performance a group of notes will take shape and become a unit that can be recognized in various pitches and timbres.

Now the question arises whether relative hearing is specifically a human capacity. Tone and the amount of noises in a sound event play a less important role in perceiving music, but more so in the allocation of environmental sounds and in understanding the human language. The differences between vowels are just a matter of overtones: depending on the position of the tongue and rounding of the lip, the tone of the voice receives a different spectrum of partial tones, different *formants*, as acousticians say. Each vowel is characterized by specific formants. So, the ability to distinguish sounds isn't specifically tailored to musical performance. Based on this analytical capability, we appreciate the sound difference between "beer" and "bear" or between "bottle" and "battle", which is rather important for communication.

Even nonhuman nervous systems are able to analyze complex acoustic signals. To distinguish the grunt of a deer from the grumbling of a bear can be vital for humans and for animals. Differentiated warning calls, food calls or mating calls can only be developed when they are well understood among conspecifics. Deceiving the great tit with a voice on a tape recorder has already been mentioned. I myself have managed several times to attract a field grasshopper by imitating their chirping. During each of my sounds the little insect hopped closer to me. Tree frogs can also be encouraged to croak by making sounds that are similar to their calls.

When analyzing sound signals, not only do noise components and the harmonic spectrum play a role: the temporal structure (rhythm) of the signal and possibly even absolute pitch also do so.

Several behavioral studies of some bird and monkey species suggest that animals, unlike humans, recall absolute pitches rather than the sound of a melody.[16]

Therefore, relative hearing seems to be a typical human ability. Is it perhaps an evolutionary adaptation in connection with our ability to speak? It seems likely, as language ability is considered *the* cognitive attribute of *Homo sapiens*. And the importance of spoken words not only depends on the type, sequence and temporal structure of speech sounds, but also on their "melody": the sentence "he is in Berlin" is a statement if the pitch falls on the last syllable, but it is a question if the voice is raised to the last syllable. In so-called tonal languages, such as Mandarin Chinese, the meaning of homonymous words differ depending on their intonation: the syllable "ma" can, depending on tone, either mean "mother," "linen," "horse" or "scolding."

Nevertheless, whether the pitch rises or falls would appear to have meaning for language competence and comprehension, but not exactly how far it rises or falls. This can be explained by the very fact that the pitch constantly changes in spoken speech and is hardly ever at a defined level, as with singing or playing a musical instrument.

But some amazing neurological findings suggest that relative hearing isn't necessary for linguistic competence: there are people that don't "understand" music and can't sing (i.e., don't recognize melodies) after damage to the brain by stroke or injury or due to a genetic predisposition. However, it isn't uncommon that their linguistic skills, including intonation, are normal. This disorder is referred to as *amusia*.[17] It is characterized by the absence of relative pitch discrimination and relates solely to processing music.

In summary: the ability to recognize and emit a musical tune, regardless of its absolute pitch, isn't just typically human, it is also a specific musical ability that cannot be explained easily by the general characteristics of hearing or by the ability to speak. Nevertheless, relative pitch isn't the only standard equipment that makes *Homo sapiens* into *Homo musicus*.

Clapping and Dancing: The Synchronous Movement

On Sunday 9th May 2010, a crammed subway car pulls into Marienplatz station in Munich. The doors open and people with red and white scarves and jerseys spill out onto the platform. Some groups of mostly young people wearing the same colors are already there, apparently in a relaxed celebratory mood, laughing, standing around arm in arm, some with a beer bottle in hand. All of a sudden, one group of about ten men and women start to sing loudly on the station platform:

> "Hurra, das ganze Dorf ist hier!
> Hurra, das ganze Dorf ist hier!"[18]

Although the song starts spontaneously and without instruction, there is no confusion. While the voices sound a little rough, but in "unison," the singers instantly agree on the rhythm and tempo of the song, whose melody, by the way, has been borrowed from the hit "Go West" by the Village People.

The jubilation is of course for the kings of soccer: yesterday, FC Bayern Munich once again became the German champions, and now thousands of fans flock together at Marienplatz to duly celebrate their team. The chants of fans have been part of soccer for decades now – their "venue" is the stadium. The music psychologist Reinhard Kopiez and musicologist Guido Brink have dedicated a book to this "FANomenology," demonstrating that the songs of the stadium fulfill almost all the characteristics of a religious cult.[19]

Another scenario, closer to the music scene: a celebrated pianist gives a rousing performance at a packed concert hall. The end of the final chord of the last piece is greeted by thunderous applause. The artist bows and leaves the stage. The applause continues and the artist comes back on stage, bows once more and receives flowers, and since the applause is still going, he soon sits back down at the piano. The hall immediately becomes silent and the artist gives an encore performance: difficult, lively piece, followed again by frenetic applause. The artist takes another bow and exits the stage. However, the audience isn't satisfied that quickly. The roar of a thousand hands suddenly becomes one rhythm, not quite synchronized at first, but within a few seconds the faster and slower claps adjust to each other: the crowd collectively produces a regular pulse, approximately 100 beats per minute. Nevertheless, it doesn't last that long because the pianist has understood the signal and appears back on stage. The enticing rhythmic clapping turns into a roaring approval. The piano virtuoso sits down at the piano and the applause dies down as he plays a *nocturne* for the final encore, understood by the educated audience as "Good night!"

What has happened? This situation is much like the singing of the football fans, a ritual in its entirety: a sequence of actions and signals of communication that progress according to certain social conventions. Communication happens without words because the participants are familiar with the meaning of the codes. These are aspects of sociology and communication studies that we can't ignore.

Behavioral scientists, however, are fascinated by the seemingly simple phenomenon that a group of individuals (which in a stadium can be thousands) can find a common rhythm within seconds without the aid of a conductor. Synchronous body movements and singing are possible because we can feel the next beat in advance. This is because the brain detects the periodic time interval between beats quickly and then times the motor commands accordingly. We don't have to respond to every single impulse. Instead, we capture the pace and adjust our motor skills to it – even if the pace becomes faster or slower.

This synchronization seems to work particularly well with a group in a euphoric mood. From birth, the body and psyche are receptive to rhythms. Babies calm down when they are gently rocked, when they sense the breathing of the mother during body contact, or if she sings to them. But the brain and body can only sway, dance, clap drum or sing "in time" to a regular beat after a few years of development. If you sing "Hop, Hop, Hop, Horsey Go Gallop" with a group of three-year-olds in kindergarten, it will turn into an odd jumble.

Now, it is time for a brief clarification of terms: *rhythm, pulse, tempo* and *time* have been mentioned. What are the differences?

The rhythm is the duration of the individual tones in a tone sequence. Let's take "Alle meine Entchen schwimmen auf dem See"[20]: four short tones (*Al – le – mei – ne*) are followed by two tones twice as long (*Ent-chen*) followed again by four short tones (*schwim – men – auf – dem*), and at the end of the line is a long tone (*See*), which lasts twice as long as *Ent* or *chen*. The notation can reproduce this rhythm like this:

♪ ♪ ♪ ♪ ♩ ♩ | ♪ ♪ ♪ ♪ ♩ |

Beat we understand as a rhythmic unit, the underlying regular impulse at equal intervals, as can be heard from the second hand of a clock, a car's indicator or a dripping faucet. One also speaks of a *pulse*, and in the theory of music from earlier centuries the human heartbeat was actually considered the basis of rhythmic measurement for music.

The quarter note (♩) in our children's song is the apparent pulse; however, it could also be the half notes (♩). In order to determine an accurate tempo for a piece of music, Johann Nepomuk Mälzel patented the metronome in 1815. It is a device operated by a spring mechanism that creates regular palpitations with a pendulum and whose speed can be adjusted as needed. Musicians use it to "keep the tempo" when practicing. In pop music, the basic beat is almost always present as a continuous beat of the drums.

People are best stimulated to clap and move along by a tempo of around 100 beats per minute. That's the "rhythm everybody wants to follow"; the speed roughly matches that of normal walking steps.[21] The majority of popular music moves in this area.

The time signature is the division of basic beats into groups, usually in groups of three or four, which consists of pronounced and unpronounced beats. In the three-quarter time | ♩♩♩ | ♩♩♩ | of the waltz, for example, the first quarter note is pronounced (heavy), the following two are unpronounced (light).

Even our everyday spoken language has a rhythm. There are long and short syllables as well as pauses of different length. If all the syllables are spoken equally long, it sounds like robot language from an old science fiction movie.

I was hired to sing in the chorus of a play at Munich Kammerspiele theatre. The director had the idea to have the hero portrayed not by a single actor, but by a choir of twelve men. Accordingly, the text the hero had to speak was declaimed by the choir. For the first reading rehearsal, the director told us to call out the verses together and, if possible, to speak naturally and not drone. We started to talk, but the individual voices fell apart immediately. We tried a few more times, but without convincing success. Through eye contact and common inhalation we managed to some extent to start together, but after only two lines everybody was out of sync again. So, why where the professionals incapable of accomplishing what soccer fans in stadiums can on the first try?

Although the text of the play is in classical verse, the "constrained" language of poetry still leaves much rhythmic freedom. The lengths of syllables and pauses and their time ratio to each other are indefinite, so each person chooses his own speech rhythm. The exact metrical orientation is missing – unlike the soccer fan's chants, which are clearly structured in eighth, quarter and half notes. Even though the director had experience with theatrical plays, he wasn't a musician. Therefore, he didn't recognize the fundamental problem and was unable to come up with the solution: either specify a precise metric of the verses (as the ancient Greeks did) or engage a conductor for the choir. This resulted in many wasted rehearsals until the members of the choir acquired the rhythm of the text through a practice-tape that had been dictated by the main actor.

The example shows the fundamental difference between a structured metrical rhythm, which most music has, and the free rhythm of the spoken language. It also answers the question of whether our musical sense of rhythm isn't simply derived from our sense of language: apparently not, as the ability to synchronize with a pulse is a specific function of the brain that clearly goes beyond what we need in order to talk and, yet, it is strongly linked to hearing. Studies have shown that it is significantly easier for subjects to tap out a basic beat to the rhythm of an acoustic signal than it is to that of a visual one, such as a flashing light.[22]

Therefore, it is perhaps not by chance that the original performance of a conductor in a concert or an opera was not only to give visible signals, but also audible ones such as stomping his foot or hitting a stick on the ground. The composer Jean Baptiste Lully hit his foot with the tip of a heavy ceremonial rod during a performance of his *Te Deum* in a church in Paris in January of 1687. Lully died three months later from an infection as a result of this injury.

As in the previous section on relative hearing, the question of evolutionary biology now also comes into play in this case: are there comparable phenomena in the animal kingdom? If so, then the ability to synchronize isn't a specific, human musical capability, but must be seen in a more general behavioral and physiological context.

In fact, neither looking to the skies nor into the oceans gives us any reason to object. Both flocks of birds and schools of fish move in perfect, somewhat weird, synchronicity. Hundreds, even thousands, of animals perform elegant movements at the same time, as if they are one giant creature. The mechanism of this phenomenon is still not completely understood. However, a significant difference between our sense of rhythm and that of birds and fishes seems to be that animals in a swarm don't follow any rhythmic signal, but are equally connected by an invisible bond when they synchronously execute the same movements. Humans are not capable of this. A horde of people push and crowd each other and will not make any headway. For synchronicity we need a metric pulse, whereas this doesn't have much effect on animals.

There are scientists who disagree on the latter point. On YouTube, you can see a video of a cockatoo named Snowball that dances to a song by the Backstreet Boys. Snowball sits on the back of a chair while the music plays, rises rhythmically from one foot to the other and makes rocking movements with its head like a teenager who wants to look cool dancing, but isn't quite sure if it really is cool. Even other animals like monkeys, dolphins and seals are known to apparently "dance" to music.

Some zoologists and neurobiologists are convinced that the ability for beat perception and synchronization (BPS) is obviously – at least to some extent – also present in other species. An interesting hypothesis states that the prerequisite for BPS is vocal learning, because those species that can dance adequately also all have the ability to imitate sounds.[23] However, if monkeys, dogs, horses or snakes "dance," then they don't do it because they react to the music, but because they are trained to perform certain movements. Our closest relatives the chimpanzees and bonobos equally have no talent for drumming or singing.

Despite all sympathy for the charming cockatoo Snowball and other swinging animals, one must recognize two things clearly. First: only domesticated and trained animals move to human music. In no case is this typical behavior of a species in their natural environment. And second: two or more animals have never been observed moving in synchronization to a regular pulse. If you were to place four cockatoos side by side on a seat back and turn on the music, you would encounter similar chaos as with the kindergarten group and the song, "Hop, Hop, Hop, Horsey Go Gallop." However, what distinguishes human musicality so crucially is the synchronization of a group of individuals.

To conclude, the perception of a regular pulse and particularly the synchronization of movements or vocal utterances to a tempo is typical to the human species. A tight coupling between the auditory and motor-driven systems in the brain occurs with this capability. The "sense of rhythm" seems to be a specific musical feature that can't be derived from the "feeling for language" or from general cognitive and motor skills. It's the foundation of musical togetherness – from a work song to dancing, to playing in a band or in a symphony orchestra. It's no coincidence that music is a contagious activity that people prefer to perform in company. There may be a very close evolutionary relationship between our musicality and our need for company.

The Human Voice

One of the greatest wonders of life that an adult will experience is when he or she looks at a baby. If it smiles, reaches for an object or even slurs unintelligible sounds, we cannot help but lovingly turn to the little person. Konrad Lorenz gave the key to this broody behavior the now proverbial name *baby schema*: a round, disproportionately large head with big eyes, small mouth and stubby nose instills solicitude. This obviously also works well with other warm-blooded vertebrates that demonstrate this behavior. Walt Disney and his artists intuitively understood to appeal to this *innate release mechanism* in their drawings: Huey, Dewey and Louie, and Bambi are typical illustrations of *baby schema*, which is why we find these characters cute and likeable. When a mother turns her attention to a baby, she talks to it in a special way. She could say, for example: "Where's the duck? There's the duck! Peekaboo! Ooh, did you make a burp? A big burp?" However, she will speak differently to other adults at the office, for example: "Where's the USB stick? Ah, there. By the way, have you finished the report for the farming community yet?"

Picture and compare both situations, slipping into the respective roles of the mother (or father) and the department manager. You may notice that not only do the words differ, but also the way you say them, the tone of your voice. In our normal everyday language the voice moves inside a relatively small pitch range. This corresponds approximately to the interval of a fifth. But when mothers and fathers talk to their babies, the voice involuntarily slides up and down much higher and lower on some syllables – this roller-coaster tonal range can measure almost two octaves. Intonation is much more pronounced and the average pitch is generally higher than in conversation between adults.

The change in manner of speech while having a dialogue with a small child happens mostly subconsciously, and it doesn't seem to be cultural, as one can find the same behavior in many different nations around the world. This way of speaking is usually characterized as "baby talk" or "infant-directed speech"; in science, the internationally accepted term is "motherese." The term doesn't mean that fathers, grandparents and nannies don't exhibit this behavior, but psychologists and behavioral scientists have naturally observed it more frequently in mothers. Many cool heads might find this way of speaking to children ridiculous. Remarkably, motherese is anything but a silly habit.

Babies accurately perceive changes in pitch and respond to melody long before they can understand the meaning of the words. So, motherese is obviously a behavioral adaptation to the baby's senses. But more about this later.

As a spontaneously occurring universal behavior, motherese shows that the human vocal range is by design much greater than the tonal range we use when speaking "normally." A healthy voice, even without vocal training, has a range of about two octaves. However, the fact that a person uses the full capacity of his vocal tract[21] when singing, but only parts of it when speaking, led biologists Mario Vaneechoutte and John R. Skoyles to the charming but equally provocative implication "We can speak because we can sing,"[25] which supports the assumptions already described by Rousseau, Heine and Darwin.

The less an organ system is "in training," the harder it is to use its potential. Anyone who for years has traveled on foot only between the armchair, car and office chair will have a hard time with a mountain hike. As a singing teacher at the university, I sometimes have to deal with young people who have almost never sung. Their voices are often aspirated and weak, and initially they have a hard time discarding their habitual pitch range. Nevertheless, with a few tricks for deeper breathing and a more favorable position of the larynx, success comes after only a short period, and it is possible to develop the voice, especially in the higher ranges, so that one can generate a voluminous sound without much effort. Only then does the natural potential of the voice become clear, though it is often hidden behind everyday speech habits.

One could say that, yes, an extensive voice is good for singing, but also for nonverbal, emotional vocalizations such as yelling, laughing and crying. This is undoubtedly true. In addition to the great tonal range, however, two other remarkable anatomical and physiological properties of the vocal tract come into play, especially while singing: the small muscles of the larynx can, in collaboration with hearing, adjust the pitch precisely along the entire vocal range. This precision engineering (also referred to as *audio-motor control*) is unnecessary while speaking, yelling, laughing and crying.

Another amazing ability is what singers call *breath support*. Unlike our closest relatives in the animal kingdom, we can produce many syllables or sounds in succession on a single exhalation. Apes cannot do that. For them the rule is: one breath, one sound. The ability to articulate during voiced exhalation is a condition of speech. However, breath support is used to an even greater extent in singing, especially when it comes to carrying high and long tones (without becoming hoarse).

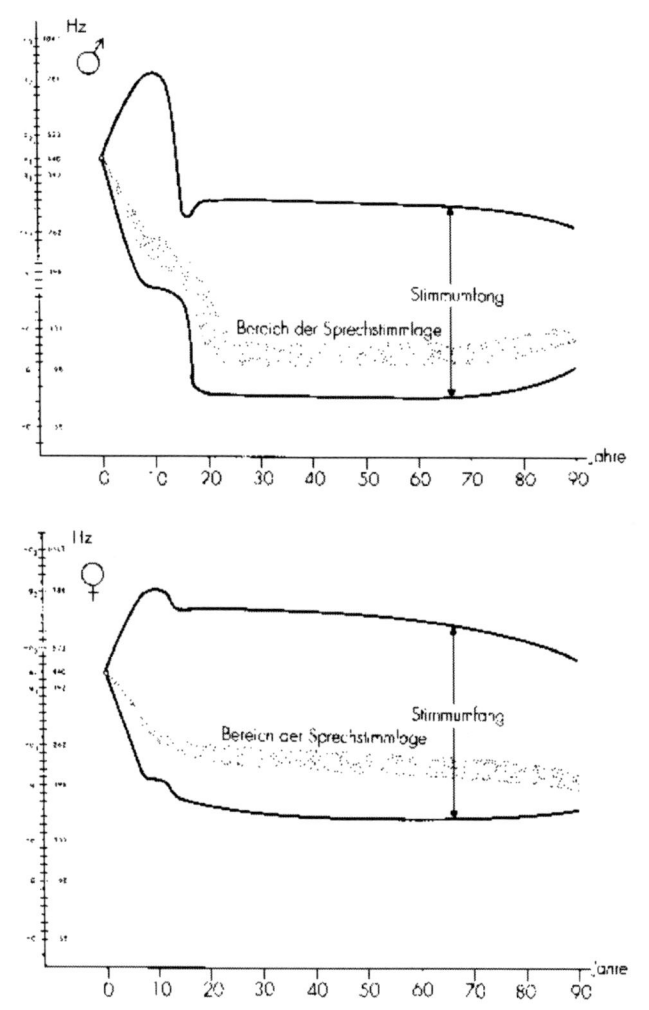

Development of the vocal range in men and women during the course of their life. (after Mathelitsch and Friedrich, 1995)

If we look at the combined capabilities of the human vocal apparatus all together, rather than considering them separately, we will see that they go far beyond the requirements of speech – especially in terms of music.

Numerous features distinguish humans from their biological relatives in the animal kingdom: the upright gait, the greatly enlarged cerebral cortex, the ability for symbolic abstraction (including speech), and many more. Some of the naturally present typical human characteristics – communicating in tones and rhythms – not only allow us, *among others*, but *mostly* designate what we perceive as "music." Music relies on three biological "pillars": the cognitive performance of relative hearing, the synchronization of cognitive-motor performance, and the anatomical and neurophysiological characteristics of the human voice.

Moreover, there are of course other characteristics that shape our musicality and are inherently present; for example, the preference for certain harmonic sounds (which mainly relies on the physics of vibrations), not to mention the desire and the strong emotions associated with making and listening to music. The mechanisms of musical perception and the effects of musical stimuli on humans have been studied quite often by musical psychologists. However, what remains unanswered is the question of what conditions in the evolutionary history of our species have shaped us into *Homo musicus*, who can master symbolic language, melody and rhythm, and is so receptive to music that it brings him joy and happiness, gives him goosebumps and can move him to tears.

The Evolutionary "Benefit"

The teachings of Charles Darwin were highly disputed during his lifetime; even today they ensure controversial, sometimes heated, discussions. It is only natural for a person to feel threatened when someone attempts to explain their nature. In Victorian England, the researcher was met by outrage over the suggested relationship between Adam and Eve and apes. Lady Ashley, a contemporary of Darwin, is said to have exclaimed about the theory of evolution: "Let us hope it isn't true. But if it is true, let's hope that it doesn't become widely known!"

After the Second World War, the social repugnance turned increasingly against the principle of *survival of the fittest* (a term that certainly didn't originate with Darwin, but with Herbert Spencer). The humanities and social sciences always had – and increasingly so during so-called postmodernism – general reservations against the undertaking to biologically justify human behavior and cultural achievements.

Evolutionary biologists typically pose the question of the "purpose" or the "benefit" of a feature: *why* does a deer have antlers and *why* do humans make music? Charles Darwin wrote initially, "As neither the enjoyment nor the capacity of producing musical notes are faculties of the least use to man in reference to his daily habits of life, they must be ranked amongst the most mysterious with which he is endowed." As already mentioned, Darwin even offers the explanation that early humans "endeavoured to charm each other with musical notes and rhythm."[26]

However, is it not too simplistic and even incorrect to insinuate that man's artistic efforts are purely for sexual purposes? Beethoven's Ninth as a mating ritual? Can culture not simply have its own purpose: *l'art pour l'art*? Cannot the secret of music remain a secret? In the opinion of cultural anthropologists such as Clifford Geertz, culture is a manmade "self-spun web of significances", levitating freely above the ground of bodily substance without being anchored to it.[27] Here, social theory goes hand in hand with Christian theology when the human spirit – and what else could art be other than a child of the psyche? – is understood to be independent from the body. The will is free; however, while human activities may be subject to social constraints, biological laws are not.

In our case, even the father of evolutionary biology himself objected, rather elegantly, that musicians may follow a purpose other than sexual promotion when they make music. But biological functions don't require conscious intention, as Darwin explains: "The impassioned orator, bard, or musician, when with his varied tones and cadences he excites the strongest emotions in his hearers, little suspects that he uses the same means by which his half-human ancestors long ago aroused each other's ardent passions, during their courtship and rivalry."[28] Now the confusion is great – it would seem the biological benefit of a behavior, not the intention, is indeed the final cause.

In order to unravel this tangle, a short excursion to the ancient Greeks is helpful, simplistic. Aristotle teaches that there are in principle four different possible answers to the question of "why." A popular example in philosophy is the question "Why does a car move?"

- A: because an engineer designed it for this (formal cause, *causa formalis*);
- B: because an internal combustion engine drives the wheels by means of a transmission (material cause, *causa materialis*);
- C: because the driver steps on the accelerator (efficient cause, causa *efficiens*);
- D: because the driver wants to go to a concert (final cause, *causa finalis*).

In fact, all four answers are correct because they designate different levels of causality. The cause Darwin's theory of evolution gives to explain a particular genetically inherited trait appears at first glance to be the final cause. Simply stated, the evolutionary explanation for why a caterpillar has the color of bark, and holds on to the ground with its hind feet and assumes a rigid body posture when it senses danger could be phrased like this: "The caterpillar camouflages itself with its color and acts like a branch to avoid being eaten by a bird. It does this in order to pass on its genes as a butterfly later in life or to preserve its species. Tree bark-colored caterpillars that become rigid when confronted by danger are better suited for survival than bright caterpillars that behave differently. The latter becomes a victim of natural selection."

Here the matter becomes unappealing, and much more so if one applies similar formulations to humans. For one, the alleged value judgment of characteristics and traits is incompatible with today's ethical views. The other issue is the "to be" formulation of the living creature's intentional action. In the caterpillar's case it is probably not true and in man's case there are obvious discrepancies between self-determined action and a suspected biological "purpose."

In fact, the statement outlined above has little to do with the scientific theory of evolution; it is a colloquial simplification. An evolutionary biologist would explain these facts to a layman as follows:

> The probability that individuals reach reproductive age with varies differently depending on environmental conditions. If there are birds that like to eat caterpillars and recognize their prey by color and movement, and if the branches on which the caterpillars reside have dark-brown bark, then caterpillars that have a bark-like color (due to random variations in their genes) and show a specific body posture are relatively rarely recognized by birds as a possible food source. The probability that a bark-colored caterpillar with a fright-rigid behavior can grow up in order to pupate and pass on their genes (in which these characteristics are also present) is under these environmental conditions relatively high. Therefore, the frequency of characteristics increases in the population and ultimately characterizes the appearance of the species.

This statement describes a mechanism that shows neither a purpose nor an objective. An evolutionary adaptation doesn't mean intent or value judgment. It is no more and no less than what nature has formed. It isn't good or bad, but it has stabilized due to a function in the maelstrom of evolution and therefore belongs to the appearance, the identity of a species.

Therefore, the evolutionary explanation model of an adaptation (or an *adaptive* trait) doesn't name a final cause (*causa finalis*), but an advanced material cause (*causa materialis*). We may reason that the misconception in perceiving the evolutionary question "why" in regard to a purpose and goal lies in the ambiguity of the words "why" and "because" (which Aristotle already knew), and our tendency to simplify matters linguistically. The phrase "The caterpillar camouflages itself *to* avoid *being* eaten" provides a description of the evolutionary process for domestic use, and shifts the light of "to be" onto an apparent intentional level, because any contrary freewill choices of caterpillars are not known to us.

In the twentieth century the theory of evolution expanded in many areas and was supported by numerous discoveries and observations. Among the most important years in the history of science is certainly the year 1953, when James Watson and Francis Crick discovered the substance that carries the information of their hereditary characteristics in all living things: deoxyribonucleic acid (DNA). The term "gene" was then given a concrete substance and has become a synonym for the biological determination of life, in natural science as well as in science-related matters.

Twenty years later, in 1973, three European scientists Konrad Lorenz, Nikolaas Tinbergen and Karl von Frisch received the Nobel Prize in physiology and medicine "for their discoveries concerning the structure and elicitation of individual and social behavior patterns": Karl von Frisch became famous for his discovery of the "waggle dance" of bees. Lorenz and Tinbergen are considered the fathers of behavioral physiology, the systematic study of the biology of innate and learned behaviors in animals and humans. This subject is also called *ethology* (not to be confused with *ethnology*, the study of cultures). More famous than the described baby schema by Lorenz is perhaps the image of the bearded Konrad Lorenz being followed by a gaggle of little gray geese who accepted him as "mother" and imprinted on him.

In the 1960s zoologist Irenäus Eibl-Eibesfeldt, one of Konrad Lorenz's students, began to apply the questions of ethology to human behavior. The research field of *human ethology* was established: which of our behaviors are innate and which are learned?

In the 1970s and 1980s, in order to explore this matter, researchers surrounding Eibl-Eibesfeldt traveled to regions of the world that had no or almost no cultural contact with Western civilization: Papua New Guinea, the Amazon rainforest and the territory of the bushmen of the Kalahari desert. The scientists filmed (often unnoticed) the everyday behavior of locals and found that an amazing number of behaviors are almost identical in their basic structure in different places around the world: facial expressions and gestures, patterns of behavior between the sexes, dealings with children, social interaction, aggression and separation. From these comparative observations and from studies of young children, ethologists deduced that the behavioral repertoire isn't only influenced by cultural learning, but is also decisively determined by biological heritage, which in turn is a result of years of evolutionary adaptation.

Evolutionary psychology, a slightly younger American branch of psychology, argues in a similar vein. It differs from the widely applied holistic human ethology mainly through the theoretical idea that the human mind and spirit exist from numerous "modules" and specific adaptations to problems that our ancestors encountered time and again during the course of evolution. These modules are responsible for individual behavioral strategies – much like the tools of a Swiss Army knife that can be folded out and used when needed.

However, in the end all these branches of science, comparative ethology, human ethology and evolutionary psychology refer back to the theory of Charles Darwin, who observations on animal and human behavior in his 1871 book *The Descent of Man*. In *The Expression of Emotions in Man and Animal*, published in 1872, he outlines the theory that the facial expressiveness in man is also determined largely by biological heritage – a thesis that was rejected for a long time and finally validated 100 years later when Irenäus Eibl-Eibesfeldt made the striking observation that children who are born deaf and blind can smile, laugh and cry like children who perceive environmental stimuli in a normal way.

Back to our original topic: music. American linguist Steven Pinker, a prominent representative of evolutionary psychology, thoroughly scrutinizes one of the sacred theories of social science in his book *The Blank Slate* (2002). It concerns the idea that man is like a blank sheet of paper at his birth – a *tabula rasa*, as John Locke formulated in the seventeenth century – where the inkjets of environment and education leave their permanent (though potentially rewritable) marks.

Pinker's counterproposal could be conveyed as follows men aren't isn't born as a blank page, but as a little book that has many words already printed on it that want to be transposed into action. His view of the *conditio humana* is based on numerous scientific facts that the guild has to offer. On the other side, according to the "Swiss Army knife" theory, Pinker concretizes why certain human strategies, likes and dislikes are the way they are and not different: because they go back to evolutionary adaptations that have been formed under the pressure of natural selection. In this context he also addresses music and explains it as follows:

> Compared with language, vision, social reasoning, and physical know-how, music could vanish from our species and the rest of our lifestyle would be virtually unchanged. Music appears to be a pure pleasure technology, a cocktail of recreational drugs that we ingest through the ear to stimulate a mass of pleasure circuits at once [...] I suspect music is auditory cheesecake, an exquisite confection crafted to tickle the sensitive spots of at least six of our mental faculties.[29]

Pinker believes that music flips certain switches in the brain, which have actually been installed for other purposes (again expressed simplistically!), especially in connection with our speech ability and control of our body movements. Pinker stipulates that music is a function that provides pleasure, just like cheesecake satisfies our ancestral hunger for high-energy nutrients, even if they're no longer necessary for our diet.

Cultural scientists and members of the educated classes who are usually opposed to evolutionary psychology can breath easy by Pinker's assessment of the phenomenon music: music is art for the sake of art and requires no biological benefits! The culinary comparison may be a little hard to stomach – not all music is sweet and fatty – but one can overlook this generalization.

However, does Pinker's view convince us know that we know how complex and specific the individual characteristics and abilities that make up our musicality are? Do we believe that Pinker's "auditory cheesecake" can have such astonishing effects on mind and body? Is it at all possible that a basically dispensable pastime could become such an integral part of all cultures, independent from each other, in different parts of the earth? Did Pinker consider that cheesecake is baked in relatively few cuisines of the world, while music exists in every culture we know of? Like the ability to speak, it is also a so-called "universal."

These questions have also been posed by other scientists, and only a few share Pinker's view. However, since the 1990s, some notable thoughts of neuroscientists, psychologists, evolutionary biologists and musicologists have found their way onto paper, recognizing (as Darwin already had) an evolutionary adaptation, a biological "benefit," in the music phenomenon: musical hunters and collectors of primitive times had more offspring than any unmusical fellow, and these offspring (i.e., us) have inherited their musicality. However, it is still debated where the biological "benefit" of music actually lies.

Lullaby in the Savannah

The clan has set up their quarters at the foot of a mountain slope. Every man, woman and older child has helped to build tents made of long wooden poles and animal hides. The tents provide shelter from the sun, wind and wild animals. The scene takes place in East Africa hundreds of thousands of years before our time, in what is nowadays called Tanzania.

In front of the clan's camp, vast grasslands extend with scattered bushes and trees. Nearby is a water source where the men wait for the thirsty antelopes, armed with stones and spears. With luck they succeed and kill an animal from which the whole clan is sated. However, most of the people feed on fruits, seeds, roots, small animals and bird eggs, which must be laboriously collected.

Vela is a skillful and experienced collector. Presently however, it has become somewhat cumbersome to go in search of food since she gave birth to her second child three months ago. The boy is healthy and is feeding well. When Vela leaves the camp she carries the baby in her arms, puts it over her shoulder or ties it with an animal hide onto her belly. Vela's older daughter is four years old and plays with the other children of the clan while her mother scrounges for food. The little one is happy on his mother's body, and when he gets hungry Vela sits down in a suitable place and nurses him.

In order to find food, Vela looks in certain proven places in the close vicinity of trees, where she collects and picks their fruits, and in some places in the grasslands where she digs certain plants' bulbous roots out of the ground. The mother can do most of it with the child on her body, but sometimes it's better for her to put the baby down for a moment – for example, when she fishes for dragonfly larvae and newts in shallow water. Today, she discovers some ripe fruit on a tree, but it hangs so high that she must climb up. She spreads out the hide she uses to collect food on the earth under a tree and places the baby on it. He doesn't like it, and as his face darkens Vela begins to sing softly. She sings the tree song, tickles the boy a bit and while she climbs up the tree to pick fruit and clean out a bird's nest she continues to sing and smile to her child who lies under the tree and watches his mother quietly.

As the shadows lengthen Vela comes back to camp. Her daughter runs towards her and hugs her, and Vela sits down with her and the baby next to the relatives at the firepit. While the grandparents roast roots and nutritious beetle larvae in the charcoal embers, Vela gives the baby her breast again. He is already sleepy and when he is finished, she rocks him gently back and forth in her arms while singing the sleeping child song.

"Ninna lulla nanna vela
Lulla ninna nanna lul"

The sister and the grandmother chime in now and then, and as the little boy goes to sleep Vela wraps him in fur-padded skins for the night. Later, she and the girl will join him, but first Vela has her hands free and can help with the preparation of the collected food. The men will also return from the hunt before the sun goes down.

Is it just a speculative story of our prehistoric time or one of the keys to the emergence of people's musicality?

Even today mothers and other caregivers communicate with babies in a musical or "protomusical" manner. Motherese, the singsong tone pitch that adults speak intuitively to babies, isn't the only common phenomenon in (almost) all cultures. Mothers all over the world sing their children to sleep. The German word for "lullaby" is "Wiegenlied" (cradle song), but lullabies also exist where cradles haven't been invented.[30] Among indigenous people, young children are usually carried on the body of the mother until they learn to walk. This is also the reason why babies of these cultures rarely cry: they feel safe and secure on the maternal body and have no reason to express displeasure. But even in a society without professional activities and strollers, there are situations in which the mother must set her baby down. This is where the hypothesis of American anthropologist Dean Falk starts off.[31]

The newborn of our earliest ancestors clung to the fur of their mother like little monkeys. However, during humanization this became more difficult, not only because the "naked ape" (as the British behavioral biologist Desmond Morris charmingly described us) has barely any fur left, but also because of his creative intelligence: this was accompanied by an increasing brain size; the larger the brain became, the earlier the baby had to come into the world in order for their big heads to still fit through the maternal birth canal, which had already narrowed due to upright walking. Therefore, human newborns, which cannot hold on themselves, are helpless "preemies" compared to infant monkeys. The human mother must hold on to her babies when she carries them around. But she can't always do that because the imaginative *Homo erectus* pursues new strategies in the search for food; they have mastered fire and may have other things.[32] So, the mother puts the baby down from time to time – and then what happens? The child cries. That shouldn't further deter the mother, she could just let it scream, finish her task and take the baby back into her arms when her hands are free (if the baby hasn't calmed down already). In fact, this strategy isn't uncommon in Western industrialized societies. What contradicts it?

Besides the fact that the persistent crying of a baby irritates not only the mother but also all the people in the area (it is a sound that immediately startles us awake from deep sleep), causes stress and could attract enemies, psychologists and behavioral researchers have found that body contact with the mother ensures that the baby builds a *secure bond*. This in turn is a prerequisite for the child to develop well emotionally, socially and mentally.

One can assume that in our evolutionary past, under the harsh conditions of a nonsedentary hunter-gatherer's life, the mothers that were content and had little stress bore the most descendants. If in turn these offspring develop into emotionally balanced, socially confident and sociable adults, then their chances to have many descendants were also good. So it is likely, as evolutionary no apostrophe state, that "evolutionary pressure" has built up in favor of behavioral strategies that establish a secure bond between child and caregiver. The main strategy is body contact during the first year of life. If that is interrupted, then the "continuum" of bonding must be maintained via different means: through the voice.

Babies respond immediately to the familiar voice of the mother – they can be encouraged or calmed down. Amazingly, they are more susceptible to singing and the intonation of motherese than to the tone of everyday language, as numerous studies show.[33]

We can conclude from these findings that the singing and chanting of a mother to her child is a behavioral strategy that is most likely *adaptive*, meaning that it is shaped by evolutionary adaptation. It fulfills the vital biological function of bonding, it is universal (observed in most cultures of the world), it is done intuitively and it addresses innate patterns of perception. In a sense, the lullaby is a musical evolution of motherese. It accompanies the child as it crosses into the dark of night, which loses its frightfulness as the child falls asleep with the knowledge that he is safe, that he is not alone. Therefore, some scientists see motherese and lullabies as one – perhaps even the strongest – evolutionary root of our music and musicality. However, this doesn't exclude other roots.

Together We Are Strong

The clan settles at a place east of the Carmel Mountains in an area that we now refer to as the land of the Bible. As the land of the Bible. A message spreads among the people of the clan, arousing fear: the people from the river behind the hill are coming, and they aren't coming as friends. They will attack us and take our caves, says the eldest, because the water has risen too high in their flood plain. They will drive us off or kill us, but keep our wives and daughters.

In the evening the men of the clan gather. They have painted their bodies and faces in the color of the wolf and drank from the war potion that is supposed to increase courage and strength. One begins to sing of brave Orkal, who was so fearless and strong he killed bears with his bare hands and defeated all of his enemies.

While some of them stay with the women and children and keep watch over the fire, a crowd of about thirty heads towards the hill. The men carry their spears and various objects made of wood and bone. From the highest point of the hill they can look down on the area of the river people on the other side. The water of the river has flooded large parts of the lowlands and glitters in the moonlight. Sporadic fires burn on the remaining dry land.

The men remain on the knoll. In the center, some start to sing huskily, a vibrant motif that is repeated constantly. Gradually the others join in, rhythmically stomping their feet, and the song gains momentum. As each man sings, he also listens to whether the voices around him sound frightened or brave; each can feel the mood of the group and adjusts his own sound to be a part of the whole. The freer and bolder the sound, the more the courage and voice of each is enhanced. Some men beat dry wood and animal bones together to the rhythm of the song, others hold horns and bison skulls to their mouths while singing so that the song turns into a wild, deafening roar that fills the whole valley of the river people. The words that the men sing gradually change, and what resounds at the end through the flood plains probably means something like:

"River people have wet feet!
Wolf people have strong teeth!"

After half an hour the singing subsides, the men calm down and head back to their camp. Two or three get the song of brave Orkal started on the way. That night their sleep is restless, but nothing out of the ordinary happens. A few days later news spreads through the clan that the river people have departed in a different direction to seek new hunting grounds.

As for the lullaby story, we don't know if this event took place quite like that. Part of the scene is based on an account in from Tacitus' *Germania* where the historian describes the *barditus*, a type of song used by German warriors to build up their courage before battle. They would also hold their shields in front of their mouths as a sounding board, making their voices resound more fully and powerfully. In Tacitus' brief description, the songs weren't so much about musical harmony, as their main purpose was to express the collective combat morale of the warriors singing them. With the sound of the *barditus*, the Germans and the Teutons prophesied the outcome of the forthcoming battle; depending on how it sounded through their ranks, they either spread terror or were themselves frightened.

In essence, Tacitus describes a kind of "feedback effect" via the sound of voices, which both indicates and influences the mood of a group, either strengthening or weakening it. a highly modern psychological observation that seems quite remarkable for a first-century Roman historian. Although Tacitus describes a farming culture that is several thousands of years younger than our speculative scenery in the Middle East, his evaluation surprisingly coincides with the thesis of two American anthropologists whose articles circulated between experts/academics a few years ago: Edward Hagen and Gregory Bryant see the evolutionary origin of music and dance in groups that convincingly represent the quality of their cohesion, outwardly and inwardly (dancing in most cultures is initially group dancing).[34] To act rhythmically is, according to Hagen and Bryant, an impressive signal that means "We're a well-rehearsed team that can act quickly and are jointly coordinated. Think before attacking and win us over as allies, instead win us over as allies!"

This hypothesis is to some extent the sociobiological answer, in a roundabout way, to more general findings confirmed by everyday experience: music not only *signals* social cohesion, it *creates* it. For warriors during the Paleolithic Age in the Teutoburg Forest and in the football stadium, certainly both apply.

However, even under less martial circumstances, people of all cultures prefer to sing, make music and dance in company. Can we detect in our penchant for musical interaction a plausible evolutionary "benefit" (to phrase the complicated Darwinian "why" once again using a simpler word), even if we dismiss the postulated signal function by Hagen and Bryant?

The success story of humans is primarily due to their social intelligence. Our ability and willingness to work together, to help one another, to distribute tasks and work towards common goals was the prerequisite for organized food gathering, for housing development, for agriculture and for the development of social communities. Those hunters and gatherers who liked to cooperate and did things together were in the long run superior to those who didn't form social groups.

Musicality could have facilitated collaboration and reinforced the willingness for it. One could initially imagine at a very basic? ergonomic level: when several people want to move a boulder or to ram a stake together, it is easier if they synchronize themselves rhythmically: *Heave ho! Heave ho!*[35] Many work songs were created in this way; for example, the song of the banana plantation workers, "The Banana Boat Song," which later became a worldwide hit by Harry Belafonte:

> Come, Mister tally man, tally me banana.
> Daylight come and me wan' go home.
> Lift six foot, seven foot, eight foot bunch!
> Daylight come and me wan' go home.
> Six foot, seven foot, eight foot bunch!
> Daylight come and me wan' go home.

However, this subject has more complex, psychological aspects to it. When people interact musically, they not only bring their movements and vocalizations together in harmony, but also their emotions. The group gets into the "mood" (the metaphor of the language here isn't by chance a musical one). This is true in our culture for congregational singing on Christmas Eve as well as in a similar manner for a school choir or a rock band, and it applies to the diverse forms of musical togetherness in other cultures: at festivals, ceremonies, rituals and at work. We must not forget that professional musicians, the stage and the audience are comparatively recent occurrences in civilization. Music was and is, in most societies, something that belongs to active collaboration in people's lives; a behavior through which they communicate with each other and which they share with each other.

Famous British anthropologist Robin Dunbar traces the emergence of language and music back through time, as our ancestors became more intelligent living together in ever increasing groups. However, the larger the group the less physical affection an individual received. Nonhuman primates maintain their social relationships in small groups by grooming and delousing each other. Our early human ancestors had to replace social body care more and more with acoustic communication. In this way they "invented" not only schmoozing and gossiping, but also the common, synchronized rhythmic singing that seems to release endorphins just as well as cuddling and grooming do, as Dunbar states.[36]

In his book *Keeping Together in Time*, William H. McNeill illustrates the eminent role of dance, but also military drills and lockstep, in all periods of human history. The cohesion of a group works best through rhythmic movement – "muscular bonding" as McNeill calls it. Again and again, we encounter this context of aggression and defense. Singing, drumming and dancing collectively can evoke strong emotional reactions, even ecstatic states, in the people involved. Eibl-Eibesfeldt points to the "sensation of being moved" that overcomes people when singing a song that means something special to the group. This may be a national anthem or even "Candle in the Wind" by Elton John.

In the last few years, several scientists have extensively studied the phenomenon of having "goosebumps" while listening to music.[37] Among other things, they were able to determine that occurrences during a piece of music that suggest a strong group presence to the listener – the crescendo of an orchestra or the sudden appearance of a chorus, for example – can cause goosebumps due to blissful sensation (which shouldn't be confused with the goosebumps of disgust that befall us when a chalk screeches across a blackboard). The euphoria created by singing and making music together results, as previously mentioned, in the distribution of endorphins, which the body also produces when we are in love.[38]

However, we only really feel the pleasure of making music together when there is interaction. Due to our musical ear and especially to our "sense of rhythm," we have a keen sense of whether the group is "together" or "apart," whether individuals listen to each other and orient themselves to each other. Thus, musical interaction shows everyone how well the group members are tuned to each other and how well-practiced they are, while it offers at the same time the opportunity to improve interaction if necessary. The positive emotions that are triggered by a successful musical interaction strengthen the social bond, reduce tension and stabilize the group. These qualities can hardly be overestimated, not only in hunter-gatherer conditions, but also in a modern community.

Even evolutionary psychology has developed, in the broadest sense, a model for the question of the adaptive significance of art that can be applied quite plausibly in this context, even if the reasoning differs a little from the previous. Our evolutionary behavioral adaptations (the tools of the mental Swiss Army knife) can be used in two ways: in case of an acute emergency (evolutionary psychology speaks of the "functional mode") or in a training run in which the behavior pattern is trained and possibly corrected (the "organizational mode"). Musical group events, where different cognitive, social and motor skills are stressed, invert be seen as a test, as a for successful management of existential problems.[39]

Whether it is this model of evolutionary psychology, the idea of social bonding or the signal theory of Hagen and Bryant that comes closest to the evolutionary truth, in our Paleolithic past, those tribes or clans (members of a village community were probably more or less closely related to each other) whose members expressed themselves musically at social events and communicated and coordinated with each other were able to make a head start on the path to the social, cultural life through their musical nature.

It is striking that one crucial factor of our lives is associated with both group music and the singing of mother and child: bonding. When people share and communicate musically they strengthen – consciously or unconsciously – their relationships with each other. A bond that begins in the family and may extend to the community or state is the building material of our social and cultural existence. It is not only anthropology that teaches teach us this, but also looking back on the millennia of human history.

Which part of musical competence is especially required in a group is obvious: the dancers, musicians and singers must perceive the underlying tempo, the pulse, and synchronize their rhythm. This ability isn't as important, for example, in the mother–child interaction. Babies cannot appreciate tempo, so the rhythm of the mother will be free and individual. In the foreground stands the mobility of the voice, far beyond the scope of speech and the sense of intonation. However, equally essential for both behavioral situations is relative hearing, the ability to capture, remember and reproduce a melody.

So, we recognize that the challenges of diverse life situations have probably caused different "evolutionary pressure" in favor of individual musical competencies, the "biological pillars" of our musicality. There isn't *one* biological necessity for *the* music, but there are a number of communicative problem-solving strategies through which we became, in the evolutionary adaptation, a *Homo musicus* or, as Desmond Morris might say, a "musical ape."

How, then, can we harmonize all these hypotheses of the biological benefits with the simple, everyday understanding that we make and listen to music simply because we enjoy it? Especially since the most biologically important behaviors are naturally equipped with strong incentives. No living entity propagates because it feels a sense of duty to pass on its own genes or to preserve its species.[40] A biological reason is no motive for action. What drives us to carry out our biological necessities are feelings of pleasure. The sex drive is the motive and the feeling of sexual gratification is the "reward," which positively reinforces our mating behavior. A comparable motivation and self-reward system acts while eating, through hunger, satiety and preference for certain taste stimuli, which are precisely those foods that are high in energy content.

The phenomenon that music can cause heart palpitations, intoxication and happiness therefore stirs up even more suspicion that we are also dealing with a self-reward system installed by evolution (again, simplistically expressed) in order to make musical behavior "tasty" to us – albeit sometimes requiring a lot of practice, patience and other investments.

We've already mentioned the linguistical danger of confusing the causes, the *causae*, in the context of the caterpillar "imitating" a branch. Behavioral biologists name the motive of an action (in this case, the pleasure that is associated with it) a *proximate* cause.[11] However, the biological benefit in an evolutionary sense is named an *ultimate* cause.[12] The proximate cause is usually obvious, but that doesn't eliminate the question of the ultimate cause. Many people dislike natural science because it threatens to take the magic out of mysterious things. As long as the moon shimmered and traveled its distant path, dreams and imagination were in good hands with it. But when astronauts left their footprints and the US flag on it and credibly reported that the previously hidden back side of the moon looks just like the front side – nothing but a dead landscape of rocks and dust – the poetic orb turned into a prosaic celestial body. Does the search for biological causes demystify the miraculous power of music? I argue the opposite is the case. If we content ourselves with the idea that music is only there for our enjoyment and has otherwise no deeper meaning for humanity, then we must, even if we love music, agree with Steven Pinker's thesis that music could ultimately disappear from the life of our species without causing radical changes in other areas, which sounds very banal and lacks mystery. If we rather follow the opinion of Friedrich Nietzsche, who said, "Without music, life would be a mistake," then that would warrant the question of why it would be a mistake and whether our need for music may have vital existential origins that are deeply rooted in our unconscious. This question enriches our understanding of the magic of sound.

Easier Sung than Said

Are the origins of music to be found in the bond between mother and child and in the cohesion of a social group? Many indications point to the fact that these two elements of life have crucially shaped our musicality. However, that's certainly not the entire explanation. All cultures have many occasions and forms of musical behavior that cannot be readily attributed to maternal affection or to the rhythmic interplay of a group. This refers in particular to situations where an individual offers something, presents himself musically, so to speak: solo performance. Again, this doesn't refer to professional musicians of our times, to the universal, possibly original forms, as they would be conceivable in our Stone Age past.

American psychologist Geoffrey Miller has an evolutionary explanation ready for the musical productivity of people which is, in every sense of the word, *sexy*. Miller believes the human penchant for artistic (self-) representation occurs because women prefer to select as a partner a man who is imaginative, creative and musical. This could have proved evolutionarily useful because these skills suggest good partner and father qualities. Those who dance and sing not only display physical fitness and body control, but also articulateness and empathy.

Miller links this hypothesis directly to Darwin, who understood human musicality as being analogous to birdsong and guessed its origin to be in advertising for partners. For Miller, the cognitive and physical skills that enable people to artistically perform are generally the result of sexual selection through female mate choice. He supports this theory with some data, especially the striking accumulation of musical productivity in men of reproductive age.

This asymmetry could certainly have cultural reasons, as Miller's data is limited to Western civilization. But even his theoretical structure is fundamentally flawed, since his theory is based on the widely accepted assumption that in the millions of years of our evolutionary adaptation, it was the men that wooed and the women that selected (*female choice*). This model explains only male, not female, creativity and musicality. Nevertheless, there is no reason to assume that women are less musical than men; after all, even the professional music scene teems with female violinists, dancers and singers. So, Miller's hypothesis can only explain part of the reality.

An entirely different – and yet, entirely plausible – approach to explaining evolutionary human music points to the possibility that there are such things as distinct female and male musicality, which may have different origins. Perhaps this difference is reflected even nowadays by the fact that certain styles of music and musical instruments are more popular with one sex than the other. A great majority of heavy metal fans are male. However, in comparison there are few male harpists. The musicologist Lorenz Welker and I have therefore proposed to unravel the much-debated question of the "evolution of music," to differentiate between diverse basic patterns of musical behavior and to separately observe communicative problem-solving strategies of musical types, which are adaptive in numerous ways and are also emotionally charged in different ways.

Statements that are reminiscent of the tender affection shown to a young child we baptized *lullaby*. Rhythmically coordinated interactions of a group, often temperamental and powerful, we called *anthem*. What the Michael Jacksons of all cultures do with music and dance received the flat description of *concert* (one could also call this *performance*). Additionally, there are other categories. The whole is a working model for human ethological analysis of any piece of music or any opera, which certainly doesn't make conventional musicologists happy.

Nevertheless, our categorization is not yet complete. Many situations cannot be easily reduced to one of the previously outlined patterns. This is especially true for all forms in which an individual has "something to say" musically.

When a priest or pastor celebrates Mass, he may implement certain parts of the liturgy either through speech or singing according to a given melodic model. In Catholic Mass, for example, the words are often sung at the end of the Eucharistic Prayer: "Through him, with him, and in him, in the unity of the Holy Spirit, all glory and honor is yours, almighty Father, for ever and ever. Amen."

Singing is an essential part of most religions. Worshippers may sing confessions or practice in common prayer and meditation. Priests, shamans and mediators between the earthly and the transcendent world sing when they proclaim words of particular importance, when they invoke the deity or conjure up spirits. Through the musical way of speaking, words from everyday language are brought out and receive special significance. The muezzin doesn't just *call* the faithful, he *sings* them to prayer.

But not only in religious contexts do people musically enhance their speech in order to communicate something of importance. In preliterate cultures, the bard – a poet and singer – was a walking history book: his job was to pass on epic reports of gods and heroes and keep the memory of people alive. At celebrations and other gatherings he presented impromptu musical epics. Young, future bards had to learn not only the stories, but also the rhythmic and melodic formulas that were to be used to compose and improvise.

Until the twentieth century, these traditions were active from Central Asia up to the Balkan Peninsula. The material we read nowadays as the *Iliad* and the *Odyssey* had already been passed on orally for centuries by many generations of epic singers and had been further developed before they were written down the name of Homer.

An epic is large in form, but we meet familiar things in miniature. In the nineteenth century, the night watchman patrolled through the city and sang the hours that the bell had struck. Even the shouts of a hawker often have a musical form. This practice has become rare, and yet still in the 1970s, on the edges of Munich, a potato dealer would travel around in his VW van, shouting through a megaphone in the village:

"Schöne neue K_{ar}toffeln
aus Neuburg an der Donau!"[43]

He would recite this in one tone and lower his voice about a third at the illustrated bottom case syllables – similar to when singing a psalm. This tone spacing is often done completely unconsciously while shouting:

"Hel-_{lo} Ja-_{mie}!"

Countless nursery rhymes and children's songs have developed out of this pattern of the "third call," as well as playground rhymes, such as this counter to an attack of character:

"I'm _{rub}-ber and ^{you're} glue,
What^{-ever} you ^{say} boun^{-ces} off^{me} and ^{sticks} to you!"

or

"I know _{you} are, but what am I?"

Otto Böckel provides a typical example of a sung ritual of dispute performed by adults:

> The opponents meet under a tree, in a tent or in a tavern. To speak in prose is prohibited to the combatants; weapons are taken away from them beforehand. Now one of the singers confronts his rival in a rhyming challenge. Many spectators stand around the singers and listen to their songs. One singer presents the other with a task he has to perform immediately in verse. Those who cannot sing the challenge on the spot will be booed and chased away, while the winner happily continues to sing and strums his guitar. The singers often pose riddles […] together, one orates it in verse, the other must immediately solve the question in the same tempo, possibly even in the same rhyme rhythm. But the assembly and its fighters are too lively for such theoretical

skills to stop there. The wine brings hot blood to boil; the singers warm up and banter flies back and forth. There is no lack of formal challenges [...], how fortunate that one has disarmed the singers beforehand for their protection. It'd be bad otherwise! Knives would speak instead of verses. An avid singer mocks the birthplace of the other – such ridicule is ancient and mocking the opponent's town is common all over the world – the attacked pays back in kind and deftly drags down his opponent's hometown. So it goes on, becoming worse and worse, in screaming and yelling rages until one falters. He must retreat under the cheers of the supporters of his enemy, but he isn't discouraged and even while in retreat, challenges the winner to a new duel.[11]

Another scene from days long gone? In fact, this event was reported at the beginning of the twentieth century in Sicily – incidentally the home of the poet Theocritus, who in the third century before Christ elevated the combative song of the shepherds to a poetic genre. Similar customs were and still are around in many cultures. They are described as a singing dispute or singing duel. Two counterparties carry out a war of words by throwing, according to certain rules, satirical verses at each other, which must be versified on the spot and presented in a song or at least a chant.[15]

In Bavaria and Austria these satires are called *Gstanzln* or *Schnaderhüpfln* and are basically comparable to modern rap battles. The singing dispute is by no means always a joking and playful matter; it can be deadly serious and even be performed for jurisdiction, as was, for example, common among the native inhabitants of Greenland, the Inuit:

> If two men had become estranged, mainly because of a woman or if an unatoned blood debt stood between them, then a matter of life and death could be decided by a singing combat. Two enemies that hadn't crossed paths in many years, who never spoke to each other and those who according to traditional obligation had to run a harpoon into their body when they met on the seas, gathered friends as witnesses and in such took care of their revenge.
>
> The listeners were then festively dressed in entirely new suits; during the summer large fleets of boats with many accompanying kayaks and during winter in jaunty sled trains. The challenge had

to be done in good time so that the opponent had the opportunity to prepare his answer, his defense and his counterattack.

The fight proceeded in a way that had the enemies lined up across from each other in the midst of the listeners; during winter in the residential home and during summer in a valley. The challenger had the first word and it was his job to sing a satirical song about the opponent to a drumbeat. Those who placed their opponent in a position so that he had the laughter on his side were chosen to be the winners with cheering cries.[46]

You might ask what this kind of folklore has to do with the singing of a priest in church, and where lies the connection to evolutionary biology. The answer may be surprising. For certain elements of behavior (especially sequences of movements) that have developed during the course of evolution into signals of understanding, ethology has found a term that originally stems from cultural studies: ritualization.

When rams butt their horns against each other during rutting season, they measure their strength, but they fight so that the opponent will not be seriously injured. Such a battle, with rules that prevent injury, ethologists call a ritual, a tournament, or a comment battle. In many animal species, males carry out animal species carry out these regulated battles where what matters is to impress, to threaten and to determine who is stronger. A credible signal makes the spilling of blood (usually) unnecessary.

Even the name in itself – ritual – shows that we humans have developed this innocuous form of arguing in culturally diverse forms. This is true for sporting competitions of all kinds; but, in a singing dispute, we can express a rudeness that would be received as a sever insult in everyday language. The prerequisite for impunity is that the participants adhere to the formal rules of the game, which are, above all: one must sing, not speak.

Generally, ritualized behavior seems to be derived mostly from actions of other functions and differs from functional movements by characteristic features: the ritualized pattern may be exaggerated and enlarged, but also simplified; it can show a "typical intensity" and thus seem quite stereotypical; and – also important – it can be repeated several times.[47] All this enables the message to "stand out from the 'noise' of other behavior" and become concise and clear for the receiver.[48]

This is exactly what happens when a priest sings liturgical words, when a bard tells of heroes or when two counterparties negotiate a dispute by means of a singing battle. These signals have a "typical intensity" because the sung speech (as opposed to everyday language) moves over defined pitches – the manner of performance is more or less set by simply structured, melodic and rhythmic models. The recitation of pitch is thus exaggerated and simplified at the same time. Not only are the musical formulas repeated many times, but so are the words. That's how they stand out from the "noise" of everyday language, attract attention and receive a special signal value. They are a confession, a call out, or as in the case of the singing dispute, ambiguous in their meaning – "inauthentic" as literary scholars call it, quite theatrically announced, but at the same time "not meant like that."

Because the criteria of ritualization are quite obvious in terms of behavioral biology, I describe spells, prayers, epics, ballads, signal calls, satires and word banter with the umbrella term, "singing as ritualized speech." However, there is a problem here: the concept of ritualization seems to imply that the functional action was there first – in our case the pragmatic "everyday" language from which the musical ritualized signal has developed. This model is not comparable at first glance with the assumption that "humans can speak because they can sing" (as Vaneechoutte and Skoyles have formulated). Now, the contradiction may be resolved if one imagines that speech and singing both arose from a common precursor, a *musilanguage*, in which the pitch had meaning (like today in Chinese).[19] Therefore, pragmatic, everyday spoken language and affective, musical, ritualized speech would then not come in succession but in juxtaposition.

There is another form of expression that is less "speech" than an involuntary emotional expression and has also been ritualized in a musical way: lamenting. The mournful song is a known practice from many cultures; it almost always pertains to a song sung by women. They lament the dead, but there are also complaints of war and hardship, of leaving the parents' home, of the loss of one's daughter by marriage and other occasions. The mourner expresses her grief and pain by a falling melody line, which is musically formed but reminiscent of involuntary crying – a musical gesture that is understood across cultures.

The behavioral idea of ritualization can provide answers to the basic question of "why" we have another "mode" of telling in addition to informative speech. However, not every form of singing is "ritualized speech." Mother–child interaction and group synchronization is easier to explain without this concept.

In this chapter we dealt with the biological foundation of human musicality. We have addressed some fairly well-defined, apparently specifically human and specifically musical characteristics that make up our "musical nature," and looked at possible reasons that these properties have developed as they have during the evolution of our species. One can deduce from this that all examples of musical behavior that we have used in this context aren't taken from our prehistoric evolutionary past, but from the present. However, when traditions are observed in similar form and with similar functions in different cultures that haven't been in contact with each other for thousands of years, then these traditions reflect with a high probability phylogenetically evolved, archaic behavioral dispositions.

Looking at this basic repertoire of musical behavior, we can see it pertains naturally to singing and rarely to instrumental music because singing is next to tapping or clapping to a rhythm – the primary, direct musical expression of people.

What is our understanding of music and the way we deal with it based on? In part, on the anthropological universals of our (musical) behavior, which all representatives of the species *Homo sapiens* largely share, whether they are Inuit, Caucasian or Bushmen. Another part of the musicality of every human is based on the "cultural superstructure" in which he feels at home, on the traditions that have differentiated over centuries and millennia in various cultural areas, depending on the geographical and social conditions.

In the following chapter, going beyond biology, we will follow the trail of cultural developments and milestones that have decisively shaped and still shape the understanding of music and behavior in Western civilization. We will focus on the European cultural history and exclude other continents – not only because this book is intended to appeal to Western readers, but also because it is exported all over the world.

II. Musical Culture

Andante ma non troppo

Mammoths, Bone Flutes and Sheet Music

After the many, perhaps confusing, answers to the question of how during evolution certain genes might have prevailed in our nature to make the "naked ape" into a "musical ape" (i.e., provided us with the skills to organize, recognize and love sounds and rhythms), we now leave the realm of biology.

Let our eyes and ears continue to trace the origin on the following pages, and bear witness to how man in Europe has dealt with musicality since early history, what was important to him in music and how it has helped shape his life and culture. In the course of doing so, it will be perhaps possible to untangle a few threads.

We linger a while longer in the Upper Paleolithic Age and re-enter the karst cave in Hohle Fels in the Swabian Alps where, 30,000 years later, archaeologists will find the little figures made from mammoth ivory and the fragments of a flute made from bone. Man, who is still in the Aurignacian period at this point, has already developed into the *Homo sapiens et musicus*, as he is now. His biological systems will change imperceptibly over the next 30,000 years. His anatomy, emotions and the abilities of his brain during the upper Paleolithic Age are the same as in the computer age; nevertheless, his experiences and his knowledge of nature, history and technology differ.

It is no coincidence that singing has been the expression of musicality most addressed in our search for the origin of music; it is the most immediate form of musical expression. Music was not invented with musical instruments. The primary musical instrument is the human body – the voice that sings and the hands and feet that clap or stomp a rhythm.

But in the cave world of the Aurignacian period in the Swabian Alps, the manmade musical instrument brought man from musical nature to musical culture. Of course, it is possible humans had already been manufacturing instruments for many thousands of years beforehand, but they so far have not been found or have long since decayed. But what the layers of earth of Hohle Fels, Vogelherdhöhle and Geißenklösterle brought forth is a wealth of objects that have so far not appeared in any of the older sites that mark the path of *Homo sapiens* from Africa through the Middle East to Europe and Asia. Some items in particular were made to represent something – especially animals, but also humans and human–animal hybrids.

It seems that man invented fine arts – the symbol – when he arrived in Central Europe here in the Swabian Alps. It is in this era of the earliest known works of art, which are several millennia older than the oldest known cave paintings in the Chauvet Cave in southern France, that the first musical instruments also emerged: flutes made of bird bones or mammoth ivory. Is this a coincidence? If not, what has a flute to do with a small mammoth ivory figurine?

The tech-savvy craftsmen of the Aurignacian period had already been carving spear points made of bone with their stone tools for many generations, but the images in their hands are something new. At first they only depict objects that play a role in the human environment, and animals are part of nature which have always been around people.

Even the sounds that humans – or animals – make with their voices are a fact of nature, and the carver can create something to emulate them: he uses his stone knife to cut a hollow bird bone in a certain way and makes holes in the tube (he may have previously done it with a reed or willow branch, but we can only speculate). Then, he puts the tube to his mouth and blows sounds with it that are like the song of a bird or even like the song that the child's mother sings for bedtime. Why the people of the Aurignacian period found it important to recreate mammoths, horses and human bodies as well as their sounds we don't know. Perhaps they believed that the hunt for the great mammoth would be more successful if they had previously touched a small replica or knocked it down with a stick. Maybe they sang magic spells during this event; maybe they played the flute to it as well. Or perhaps the small, round figurines were nothing more than toy animals for children. We only know one thing: the representation and imitation of the environment, the invention of the *artificial*, the *to-act-as-if*, is in the original sense an element of imagination and a sense of design, the nucleus of civilization.

Wind instruments from the Stone Age have survived for thousands of years and have now been brought to light. These "tools," which imitated human vocal sounds or the sounds of animals, were carved from bird bones or the tusks of mammoths. Bird bones are the ideal material since they are hollow: the forearm of a swan's wing is a thin tube that only needs to be cut to the proper length and fitted with finger holes. It takes much more work and time to carve a flute from ivory: a straight rod must be obtained from the curved tusk and split longitudinally; the two halves must then be hollowed out and glued back together again, forming an airtight seal.

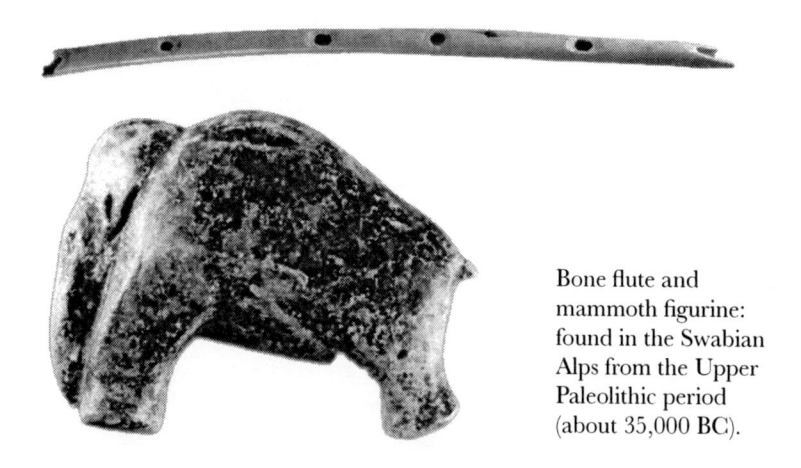

Bone flute and mammoth figurine: found in the Swabian Alps from the Upper Paleolithic period (about 35,000 BC).

In these simple flutes (much like those used in our time, for example, by pastoral people of the Mediterranean and the Near East) a sound is produced when air is blown over the cut edge of the opening and starts to vibrate in the tube. If the player closes and opens the finger holes with his fingers, the vibrating air column is shortened or lengthened and the sound becomes higher or lower.

Engineer and archaeologist Friedrich Seeberger has experimented with creating and playing exact duplicates of the brittle Stone Age flutes from the Swabian Alps. He found out that it is, in fact, possible to extract sounds from the small instruments. The result is recognizable in children's songs such as "Laterne, Laterne, Sonne, Mond und Sterne," but we also know it from traditional East Asian music: the pentatonic scale. The spacing of the finger holes is not by chance. It's consciously chosen so that the sounds of the flute form harmonic vibration ratios.

Another musical instrument that was played in the traditional cultures of the Old and New World for thousands of years is the so-called musical bow. Its construction differs little in principle from the hunting bow from which arrows are shot; it may have even emerged from it. Musicologist Curt Sachs, best known for his systematic classification of musical instruments, asked in 1929,

"What was more natural than to make the hum of a quick snapping back tendon to express themselves? Didn't the hunters have to perceive random sounds; didn't they have to get hold of the natural order of things and use it?"[1]

The string of the musical bow can be plucked, struck, brushed or even blown. In many cultures the bow is played as a "mouth bow," meaning the player places the string or the bow rod in his mouth so that the sound is amplified by the resonance of the oral cavity.

We cannot determine whether string music was in fact "discovered" at the same time as the bow and arrow, though a close relationship with hunting is often, but not always, recognizable. A 15,000-year-old rock painting in the cave of Les Trois Frères in southwestern France shows a man in a horned animal mask who is apparently playing on a mouth bow to beseech what looks like two fleeing animals, a deer and cattle – perhaps it is hunting magic. The Khoisan of Southern Africa play music on the same bows they shoot with. Other cultures that do not hunt with the bow and arrow still know of the musical bow. Some cultures on the African continent even considered the musical bow to be solely a woman's instrument to accompany lullabies or songs of longing for the beloved. A hunter would never play it.

What can we learn from our first stop on the journey through the history of musical culture? Professor Nicholas Conard, director of the excavations at the caves in the Swabian Alps, concludes from the discovery in the Hohle Fels area that bone flutes were used in the Stone Age "in everyday life and not only in specific, for example, ritual contexts." This ascertainment is noteworthy: religion, rituals and magic gave rise to singing, dancing and playing musical instruments from the beginning. The "magician" or "shaman" of Les Trois Frères points to this, as well as the dancing people that can be seen in numerous other petroglyphs. Conard emphasizes that a flute made from ivory, in contrast to a flute made from bird bones, must have been something special because production required technical perfection and a great deal of time, and also because ivory was the most beautiful and valuable material known.[2]

Even in "Stone Age" cultures, music was part of something special, in sacral events and festivals as well as in everyday life.[3] This applied to singing in any case; the musical bow, in its simplicity and in its relationship to the hunting bow, was rather a device of everyday life than a sacred object.

With the invention of "tools" that allowed people not only to imitate the sounds of nature with moving air and vibrating strings but also to create new sounds, music detached a little from the phylogenetically evolved contexts of communicative behavior. In contrast to the voice, the direct expression of human nature, a musical instrument was an object. Its importance became symbolic. The function of musical behavior became more diverse and took on a life of its own – not least because of the pleasure that making music naturally gives us. This does not mean that the roots of the evolutionary "why" have disappeared. They are part of our genetic heritage, deeply embedded in the subconscious, but can't be recognized in some places right away because culture has outgrown it.

One novelty of instrumental music we take for granted nowadays is that of sounds without words. Singing was indeed initially a musical way of speaking: people of primitive cultures sang words without an exact linguistic meaning, but they hardly ever sang tones without any text. Vocalizing, singing in one vowel, only became pedagogical practice in Europe in the eighteenth century; later on Sergei Rachmaninoff raised it to the level of art, where the voice mimics the wordless instrument, thus imitating the imitation.

Last but not least, singing works without music theory. When we move the voice from one note to the next we don't measure the ratio of the vibrations beforehand in order to strike the right note. Our innate sense of harmony, the inherent order of tones, takes care of that automatically. It is different when one constructs a musical instrument.

We can try to build a simple flute ourselves, similar to that found in the caves of our Stone Age ancestors. In absence of bird bones we work on a piece of bamboo or a hollow branch, cutting a straight edge at one of the open ends and then carefully drilling finger holes in the tube. If we successfully elicit sounds from this instrument, we will notice that the height and distance of sounds that can be blown on the flute are determined by the length and diameter of the tube and the spacing of the finger holes. If we want to play different melodies in another tone scale then we must change the design, most likely choosing different spacing of the finger holes. If we have the time and patience for it, we can make several attempts until our ears like the sounds.

The Stone Age instrument-maker had to "measure" by trial and error how far the finger holes had to be spaced for a given thickness and length of tube so that a particular series of tones was playable. Also, in the case of the musical bow, there is a direct relationship between string length, tension and pitch – a long string sounds deeper than a short one. If the string is tightened, the pitch rises; when loosened, the pitch decreases.

Anyone who builds a wind or string instrument will inevitably recognize the fundamental relationships between size, number of finger holes or strings, and sound. Music theory began with the invention of musical instruments – many thousands of years before it was written down.

Size and Number, Harmony and Character

Everyone should remember the name Pythagoras from mathematics classes at school. The Greek philosopher, who lived in the island of Samos in the sixth century BC, is ascribed the theorem on the relationship existing between the sides of a right triangle: the square of the hypotenuse is equal to the sum of the squares of the two other sides $a_2 + b_2 = c_2$. We will want to leave this brief reminder behind with the compass, protractor and blackboard chalk; however, remember that the Piythagorean theorem is the result of the endeavors of the philosophical school of Pythagoreans to capture the world with dimensions and numbers. This may sound a bit dry, but behind it is a spectacular idea and a holistic view of the world – today we would probably say it is an "interdisciplinary approach."

Pythagoreans not only recognized that the dimension numbers 3, 4 and 5 describe the sides of a right triangle (since $3^2 + 4^2 = 5^2$). They also discovered that the division of the string of a musical instrument can create, in relation to small integers, tones that sound harmonious to our ears. Pythagoras and his followers explained the basis of all subsequent harmony: strings whose lengths have a 2:1 ratio sound in an interval of one octave. The ratio 3:2 results in a fifth, the ratio 4:3 results in a fourth, which is followed by a major third at 4:5 and a minor third at 5:6. The fifth is the building block with which all tones of a scale can be constructed.

However, a misunderstanding can easily arise: in ancient Greece, "harmony" means the ratio of *successively* sounding tones. The "vertical" theory of harmony of simultaneously sounding tones is a modern development. The ancient Greeks most likely did not know polyphonic music as we understand it.

According to legend, Pythagoras discovered the relationship between sound and number as he passed by a blacksmith and heard the sound of impacting hammers. Amazed by their different harmony, he weighed the hammers and recognized by their weight ratios the proportions of musical intervals. It took more than 2,000 years until Marin Mersenne pointed out in 1636 that this narrative was physically incorrect. However, the Pythagoreans correctly recognized the relationship between interval and string length. Today we know that these number proportions and the ratio of frequencies describe the number of vibrations per second (which ancient Greeks could not measure).

"The essence of things lies in the number." Pythagoras' followers assumed that the proportions of small integers were also realized in the orbits of heavenly bodies: according to the Pythagorean view, planets' movements follow the same mathematical laws as the strings, creating a *Musica universalis* (universal music or music of the spheres) – a form of music imperceptible to the human ear.

Since music reflects the order of things in dimension and number, music theory was regarded in the Middle Ages as one of the "seven liberal arts" arithmetic, geometry, astronomy and music (which form the *quadrivium*, the "four-way" from which the natural sciences emerged in modern times), and grammar, rhetoric and dialectic (the *trivium*, the "three-way" of the language arts). Later on, today's humanities emerged from the *trivium*, and the adjective "trivial" is derived from this term.

According to the holistic doctrine of the Pythagoreans, not only are movements of cosmic and earthly things ordered by dimensions and numbers, but the movements of the human soul should also obey the laws of harmony that are audible in music. From this world view it can be easily understood that music must have played a prominent role in the social life of ancient Greece, in particular in education and in building the character of youth:

> Then, again, the teachers of the lyre take similar care that their young disciple is temperate and gets into no mischief; and when they have taught him the use of the lyre, they introduce him to the poems of other excellent poets, who are the lyric poets; and these they set to music, and make their harmonies and rhythms quite familiar to the children's souls, in order that they may learn to be more gentle, and harmonious, and rhythmical, and so more fitted for speech and action; for the life of man in every part has need of harmony and rhythm.[1]

The piecemeal doctrine of the Pythagoreans that certain tonalities and rhythms are, according to their nature (*ethos*), "in tune" with the character of people is taken on by Plato (427–347 BC), who in turn brings to mind the music theorist Damon of Oa.

To gain a little insight into the contemporary debate on educationally valuable and less appropriate music, we follow a short dialogue on musical education that Plato conveyed in *The Republic*. We hear from Socrates, Plato's teacher, as well as Adeimantus and the musician Glaucon:

> "And again, the music and the rhythm must follow the speech."
> "Of course."
> "But we said we did not require dirges and lamentations in words."
> "We do not."
> "What, then, are the dirge-like modes of music? Tell me, for you are a musician."
> "The mixed Lydian," he said, "and the tense or higher Lydian, and similar modes."
> "These, then," said I, "we must do away with. For they are useless even to women who are to make the best of themselves, let alone to men."
> "Assuredly."
> "But again, drunkenness is a thing most unbefitting guardians, and so is softness and sloth."
> "Yes."
> "What, then, are the soft and convivial modes?"
> "There are certain Ionian and also Lydian modes. that are called lax."
> "Will you make any use of them for warriors?"
> "None at all," he said; "but it would seem that you have left the Dorian and the Phrygian."[5]

The term "key" here actually means "scale type," what we distinguish today with the terms major or minor. In ancient times (and the Middle Ages), we didn't simply divide them into two scale types with a typical melodic character, but at least seven, designated with names of various tribes: the Dorians, the Phrygians, the Lydians, etc. This makes the conversation more understandable, and yet it appears a little bizarre nowadays. Whether the Lydian key actually makes young men effeminate or if the Phrygian key actually makes them brave we can scarcely comprehend today; although the signature of the key is transmitted to us, the characteristic melodies and rhythms are not.

Does the music theory of ancient Greece have a meaning for our present understanding of music and how we deal with it? Were the holistic ideas of the Pythagoreans purely esoteric, or did these philosophers find, over 2,500 years ago, such a thing as a musical world formula?

According to current astronomical knowledge, the movements of heavenly bodies do not produce heavenly sounds. However, the ancient idea of *musica universalis* is not completely grasped out of thin air. Johannes Kepler, one of the founders of modern astronomy, proved in the seventeenth century that orbits and orbital periods of planets – as the Pythagoreans had described – stand in similar harmonious proportions to each other as consonant tones. It is no coincidence that Kepler named his scientific masterpiece *Harmonices Mundi* (1619), the "world harmony." Harmonious proportions seem to be found in the biggest and smallest things.

Music lessons in ancient Greece. Attic red figure vase-painting, around 510 AD.

Those who watch nature with open eyes recognize the numbers four and five, or the regular spiral construction of flowers, or marvel at the snowflake's six-pointed star shape. Modern physics teaches that the building blocks of matter, for which Plato's contemporary Democritus already postulated the term *atomos*, the "indivisible," are inconceivably similar to small solar systems. The nucleus is surrounded by electrons whose spheres are only stable by certain constellations of numbers.

The idea that the world is sound belongs to the realm of the esoteric because no physical connection exists between planetary movements, flower structures or sound waves, the ordering of the macro- and microcosmos by dimension and number is not imaginary.[6] One just needs to pay a little attention not to mix one's organizing principles with romantic enthusiasm. The proportions of small integers such as 3:2 or 4:3 are something other than the famous "golden ratio" or the related sequence of Fibonacci numbers (0, 1, 1, 2, 3, 5, 8, 13, 21...), which can be recognized in leaf growth and inflorescence in many plants. The golden ratio *cannot* just pose as a fraction of integers. Therefore, an interval of two frequencies set to the golden ratio sounds off to our ears.

The decisive factor is the realization that our senses are adapted to the dimensions of nature. We can intuitively evaluate organically grown structures as "beautiful" because our eyes like the proportions of the golden ratio. In contrast, our hearing is tuned so that we can perceive two sounds more "consonantly" the simpler their vibration ratios, as Pythagoras formulated. The 2:1 octave is the most consonant interval, followed by the fifth with 3:2, the fourth with 4:3 and so on.

Today we know that these tones are "related" to each other by their sound spectrum: every musical "tone" – whether it's based on a piano string or human vocal cords – can be divided into a series of elementary vibrations whose frequencies are integer multiples of the fundamental frequency. This series is called a *harmonic* or *overtone series*. A string that is tuned to a C3 produces not only this one sound as a keynote, but above it sound the C4, the G4, the C5, the E5, the G5 and more overtones – which are the vibrations of half, a third, a fourth, a fifth, etc. of the string length. Tones with consonant intervals have one or more of these overtones in common.[7]

The proportions theory and physical findings are confirmed by the psychology of perception: 75 percent of listeners who are not musically trained perceive the interval of an octave as one single tone. With a fifth it is still 50 percent, a fourth 33 percent and a third 25 percent. The more consonant simultaneously sounding tones are the more people hear them as one single tone. The more dissonant the interval, the easier it is to recognize two different tones within.[8]

It's no coincidence that the findings the Pythagoreans 2,500 years ago are now the basis of European theories of music and harmony. More still, the strict orientation of European music to the theory of harmony between 1600–1900 is probably the main reason why "classical" European music has enjoyed such amazing success outside of Europe (and its "Colonies," North America and Australia). Music students in Japan, China and Korea do not engage in traditional Asian music, but instead primarily study Vivaldi, Mozart and Schumann. Critics like to call this cultural imperialism, but it is certainly no coincidence that in the highly successful "classical" music of Europe, consonance is the musical "home" and dissonance is always a short distance away from home. Of course, Anglo-American pop music is a global phenomenon, and its architecture relies even more than classical on consonance and rhythmic regularity.

In contrast, modern "classical music" of the twentieth century deliberately breaks off the relationship with consonance. Arnold Schönberg, one of the founders of atonality, stated,

> The terms consonance and dissonance, which designate a contrast, are false. It only depends on the growing ability of the analyzing ear to familiarize itself with the distant overtones and to use them to expand the concept of artful harmonic sounds in such a way that it can accommodate the entire inherent phenomenon. What is remote today may be near tomorrow; the only thing important is to be able to get closer.[9]

Schönberg was proven wrong. Even after a century of musical avant-garde, atonal music was never really accepted by the majority. Our spirit is indeed willing to learn, flexible and curious, and there are certainly people who would rather listen to Schönberg than Mozart. However, this cannot be generalized. A big concert hall cannot be filled with twelve-tone music alone. Therefore organizers, who must not only think of the aesthetic education of the people but also about money, will first play a modern composition and then a popular romantic piece for an evening's program. However, the actual "modern" music for most people is pop music – which certainly isn't a judgment of quality, but a notable finding. But more on this in Chapter IV. Musical perception is based upon the acoustical conditions, as Pythagoras had already discovered.

What else have we learned in our stay in ancient Greece, aside from the laws of musical harmony? Let us look a little bit around before we continue on our journey.

The Athenian civilization handled music on different levels, which penetrate and fertilize each other. The cosmological ideas of the Pythagoreans are probably on a very intellectual and esoteric level, but musical practice can reap the benefits of this thinking too. From a moral perspective the ideas of Damon and Plato flow into a specific concept of music pedagogy that apparently – at least in classical times – was also being implemented into practice. Several vase paintings showing how boys were taught a wind instrument while playing the lyre and sometimes also an Aulos. Music education is of great importance to the Greeks, not so much as education *of* music but rather education *through* music. According to philosophical considerations, musical practice is a way for the holistic education to raise responsible people that can also become more skillful in "speech and action."

One might read something similar in a recent newspaper article. Music education promotes the personal development and social skills of children – these are the key words of current research and policy in music pedagogy! All of a sudden ancient Greece appears very modern.

For Plato, the relationship between music and society must have been obvious in his time: from his vantage point, the culture and democracy of the Athens city-state flourished during Damon of Oa's lifetime. He himself observed, only a few decades later, how the city-state was rocked by political turmoil, while music became more and more popular for entertaining large audiences, which led to actual musical activity being forgotten. It is understandable that the philosopher warned people about the new developments in musical culture in his country and brought Damon's thesis back to mind: "For the modes of music are never disturbed without unsettling the most fundamental political and social conventions, as Damon affirms and as I am convinced."[10] Incidentally, what is remarkable about this thesis is also the blatant contradiction to the previously cited view of the American Steven Pinker: "Music could vanish from our species and the rest of our lifestyle would be virtually unchanged."[11]

The holistic meaning of music for the individual and for the community is expressed in ancient Greece not only in the curriculum, but also in many areas of social life. That music accompanied sports, for example, is self-evident. Images of various competitions often show athletes and aulos (a wind instrument) together, most often with the aulos player next to a discus or javelin thrower.[12] So musical and gymnastic exercise are directly related; athletes performed their movements in unison with music (in our time this only applies to figure-skating or in some freestyle disciplines such as dressage). Music not only accompanied athletic competitions, it itself was also a competitive discipline. It was *Greece's Got Talent* at the Pythian Games, as Greece looked for a "super citharode" (a citharode is a singer who accompanies himself on the cithara); however, the task was not – as in today's time – to demonstrate the repertoire of other composers, but to represent one's own poetry. Singer, composer and poet were one and the same person.

Music was also indispensable at parties. Women playing the aulos and singing drinking songs would accompany a feast; and at various festivals of public life the chorus played an important role. Even the classic tragedy found its origin in the parades that were held in honor of Dionysus, where revelers dressed as goats would sing in chorus to the god of wine and fertility and dance to the music of the aulos.

The com-penetration of Greek life and music of Greek life with music is also reflected in Greek mythology, which tells us why ancient Greek musical culture was divided into something like classical and popular music. The miraculous feat of strength with which the newborn child-god Hermes created the lyre suggests the particular importance of this instrument. Apollo became the god of music, conducted singing muses and gave string music to the spell-singer Orpheus. Thus, the lyre must be an instrument of higher, cultured, ethically valuable music and therefore particularly suitable for the education of youth. It is likely not by chance that Apollo was also an excellent archer. Elsewhere, Homer even reports that Diana, the goddess of the hunt, inspired her twin brother Apollo to create the lyre with her bow, whose sound flatters the ear. So, the myth casually reminds us of the ancient connection between string instrument and the hunting bow.

The counterpart to the parent Apollonian sphere is the animalistic, oppressive environment of Dionysus. His instrument was the aulos, a reed instrument, which suited the loud, nasal, penetrating sound of hooved satyrs and boisterous drinking. When Athena saw her reflection on the water's surface playing the aulos, she was troubled by her ugly, inflated cheeks and angrily threw the instrument away. It was found by Marsyas, a satyr. He was thrilled to play it and unfortunately entered into a musical contest with Apollo. Inevitably the satyr lost against the string-playing God and was even skinned as punishment for his arrogance.

The lyre's image in ancient Greece was approximately that of the piano in the educated German bourgeoisie of the twentieth century.

The aulos was something more like saxophone or electric guitar. But the use of the aulos in sports and at work (vase paintings also show this) proves that the instrument did not belong exclusively to the drunken ecstasy of Dionysus, but in a more general sense also to the physical, natural side of people. Aristotle, a more liberal thinker than Plato, essentially shared the teachings of the ethos of harmonies, but also applied music to relaxation and the entertainment of audiences, for which the "orgiastic" aulos was the correct instrument.[13]

The polis of Athens – a highly advanced, literate civilization with a differentiated society, urban infrastructure, schools, science, administration, temples and specialized professions – was also a musicalized civilization. That much you do not learn in history class. This is what connects us today to ancient Greece: their mythology, the political system, philosophy and science, the theater, and last but not least, the holistic (mental and physical) education of people – all this was interwoven with various forms of music.

Apart from the distinction between classical and popular music, which is hinted at in ancient Greece, we can discover two forks of musical culture in ancient times that are probably indicative of all civilizations (at least to some extent). Firstly, musical pursuit became a profession – not generally, but increasingly. This presupposes that there were people who *let* others sing and play rather than doing it themselves and were willing to reward music as a service (which Plato was critical of). The branching off of professional music from general music eventually led music to disengage itself from functions, so that it was to be listened for its own sake. The songs that transported the epic, the aulos that accompanied athletic competition and the lyre with which boys practiced moderation were all means to an end. In the presentation before an audience, the music became an end in itself. The evaluation of this end in itself may change with time. Plato criticized it as a loss of meaning, though Aristotle had no objections. Influential music critic Eduard Hanslick stated in the nineteenth century that the emancipation from the outer purpose was the condition that transformed music into "musical art."

We must not forget that, in addition to the academic and popular music of the city, the archaic folk music of shepherds and peasants was also lively, as in all preliterate pastoralist and agrarian cultures. But even the simple reed flute deserved a creation myth in the history of the demigod Pan and nymph Syrinx. However, the relationship between Theocritus' bucolic poetry and Homer's epic and the simple impromptu singing of shepherds from Asia Minor and the Balkan Peninsula is quite a close one. American Milman Parry discovered around 1930 that this orally given, improvised verse similar in shape and construction to that of Homer, and thereby placed the philological, idealized image of the father of poetry on its head. So let us write in our travel diary under "ancient Greece" the motto: music differentiates head and heart, but educates the whole person and connects heaven and earth, whereby heaven, as well as the planets, is also referred to as the gods.

Singing for the Heavens

In the sixth century AD, the son of a Christian Roman patrician was enjoying a rising political career family at a young age. Born 480 AD in Rome, he became senator in the first years of the sixth century ans *sole consul* in 510. His name was Anicius Manlius Torquatus Severinus Boethius. In 522 he was appointed counselor at the court of the Ostrogothic king Theodoric in Ravenna, but his fortunes turned abruptly the following year: Boethius was implicated on false charges in a trial for treason and imprisoned. In prison, he wrote his treatise *De consolatione philosophiae* (*The Consolation of Philosophy*), before he was executed around 525 on Theodoric's orders.

The musical significance of this educated man with a tragic fate is that he reworked ancient Greek music theory into Latin as a Christian scholar and passed on the work *De institutione musica* to the Middle Ages. In the cultural catastrophe of the Migration Period, in which not only the heads of marble statues but also the traditions of thought were broken, this transfer of knowledge was astounding.

In subsequent times, scholarly monks in the monasteries all over Europe built the system of Christian church music on the foundations of second-hand ancient music theory and Jewish psalmody. Even the musical ethos of Plato was picked up. As in ancient Greece, the Middle Ages knew several tone genders or modes; however, due to a misunderstanding in the transference, these "church tone types" were not identical to their homonymous ancient Greek role models, and medieval music theorists did not agree on which modes expressed or evoked which effect (melancholy, combativeness, cheerfulness, etc.).

This uncertainty may be proof in modern musicology that medieval music theory was nothing more than speculation. However, for the even-more-modern field of cognitive psychology these differences are only logical: the emotional response to certain musical stimuli cannot be generalized, but depends on the personality of the individual. But the opinion that there is a basic musical ethos – even if one cannot agree on determining it universally – is not only culturally and historically interesting, but psychologically realistic.

Church music in the Middle Ages initially consisted only of unanimous singing without the accompaniment of instruments. Today this music is called *Gregorian chant*. It is said that Pope Gregory the Great collected and arranged the tunes in the sixth century, though this is probably legend. For a long time there was no accepted sign system for writing down the music. Isidore of Seville, a contemporary of Pope Gregory, stated, "If the tones are not retained in people's minds they will die because they cannot be written down." Therefore, the repertoire of chants for Mass and hourly prayers was passed down orally in monastic singing schools, and memorized through singing auditions and recitals. The repertoire was thereby not static; it was constantly extended with new forms. Because of the lack of clarity in the transference from mouth to ear to mouth, different regional versions of songs were created.

Therefore, the concern that the melodies would be lost and the need for liturgical unity in the Church inevitably lead to the development of a script that was not only fixated on the words but also on the way they were sung. It began with graphical signs that somewhat represented movements of tones, but didn't depict exact intervals. These signs were later called *neumes*.

A Benedictine monk from northern Italy would later make two simple yet epochal inventions, changing the course of European music history. One made it possible to accurately write down music and read "from a sheet," the other made it significantly easier to convey it orally. Around the year 1000, Guido of Arezzo placed the *neumes* on a set of lines whose spacing was a third, so that notes were not only represented by a place *on* each line but also *between* them. At the beginning of the line system was a "key" that indicated where the C was located. Thus, musical notation was invented. It was developed further – in particular the addition of designated tone duration was added later – but modern notation was, in principle, Guido's idea. But he also knew that music is better learned through listening and singing than by reading, so he invented a way to sing the notes of a melody so that the pitches could be identified when in doubt (such as when a cantor intones uncleanly): the syllables *do re mi fa sol la*. Each of the syllables belongs to a step of the scale and the step *mi-fa* (in C major it is E-F) designates the semitone (the seventh step *ti/si* was added later). The syllables are easily singable and can be clearly distinguished acoustically, and they designate (other than C, D, E, etc.) not necessarily absolute pitch, but levels of a system that can be moved up or down depending on the vocal range. Even today, this *solmization* represents in many countries, in Latin and Eastern Europe more so than in Germany, the foundation of music education. The Italians talk of of *solfeggio*, in French it is called *solfège*.

Guido's invention of musical notation is around 1,000 years old. What does that mean for the progress of European music? Almost everything, one must probably reply, that we now associate with the realm of "classical" music, with music history, music education and musicology. Through notation the fleeting is retained; a momentary, fading performance becomes a lasting, portable and repeatable piece (a similarly important revolution in music wouldn't follow until about nine hundred years later with the invention of the phonograph).

The musical document is supposed to capture the essence of the song. The more accurate the information, the closer one interprets the text, the less the need – or possibility – for the interpreter to create something new, of his own, in the moment; deviation from the notation is regarded as an error.

Only through the literacy of music does the composer exist. Authorship in Latin is called *auctoritas*: the "authority" lies with the person who has written the piece, not with the one who reiterates it. This contrast between the learned *musicus* and the inferior *cantor* was not only emphasized time and again in the Middle Ages, but our current concept of the "score," the core of modern music history and musicology, is also based on it. The composition in the form of notes is the "score" of the composer. A performance is considered successful if the musicians play the music "according to the score," implementing the notation as accurately as possible in order to truly fulfill the will of the composer.

One seemingly obvious feature of our music today has about as long a history as the notation: the polyphony. This is no coincidence. The complex architecture of superimposed, rhythmically independent voices requires a construction plan. This does not mean, however, that it would be impossible to sing and play polyphonic music in an oral tradition. Two voices, which don't require notes, may develop from the unison: one voice plays a tune while a deeper, continuous tone and sometimes the fifth are held below it. The bagpipe is one such example. According to certain rules and experience, singers can sing a harmonious second or third voice that fits the melody, off the cuff. Bavarian three-voiced singing, a folk art, is wonderfully accomplished. However, a polyphonic motet by Palestrina or a fugue by Bach would not be possible without notation.

There is little doubt about the epochal progress created by Guido of Arezzo, in his time, and the development of composition in the following centuries. But all this is just one side of music's life. The music that was recorded in writing during the Middle Ages and therefore transferred to our time was initially only the music of worship. The Church had a monopoly on education; the learned *musici* were monks. They relied on Boethius in their emphasis on the priority of music theory before music practice. The doctrine of monastic schools defined music as a technical and religious exercise – a historical "invention" even. A music textbook from the eleventh century begins with the following dialog: "Who invented music? - Pythagoras, the great philosopher. - How was music invented? – Through the sound of hammers!"[14]

The heavenly harmony, which, according to the opinion of the Christian Middle Ages, Pythagoras found by God's will was also revealed in plainchant which the Holy Spirit himself whispered in the form of a dove to Pope Gregory the Great. Depictions from the High Middle Ages and later periods show Gregory with a white dove on his shoulder with its beak to his ear as the Pope writes in a book – a symbolic picture because musical notation was, as is said, still not known in Gregory's time.

The selective tradition of ancient music theory, the claim to power of the Church over music and the concentration of education in the monasteries are the reasons why musical erudition in the Middle Ages almost exclusively fixated on church music, on the function of singing during Mass. Even ancient Greece defined music as educationally valuable while at the same time writing about the connection between the singing matches of shepherds and the playing of the lecherous satyr's flute to the pantheon. However, medieval academia acknowledged that the phenomenon was not music in its entirety. Book illustrations and sculptures show us exactly how sacred music was separated from the secular music of the minstrels, jugglers and dancers, how the minstrel lured evil snakes with his reed pipe that would crawl into the poor sinner's ear. The odor of the Dionysian aulos still surrounded wind instruments and instrumental music had no place in churches for centuries instrumental music had no place in church.

Vienna Gregor plate, ivory carving, ninth century.

That changed in time. The first to appear as a companion to the choir was the organ (which, of course, the ancient Romans already knew), and other instruments gradually gained admittance to church music. The monasteries succeeded to gradually lighten the negative attitude towards musical instruments, which could be related to the fact that even clerics took pleasure in musical craftsmanship and they themselves engaged minstrels for entertainment.

As with chivalry in the Middle Ages, secular love poetry came into fashion and the art of the troubadours and minstrels flourished; erotic songs and Christian devotions to Mary prevailed. From this time on there are more and more written records of the court's art of poetry and music, and the melodies of the vernacular love songs were often the same as those of ecclesiastical Latin chants.

With the strict separation of these areas, theory and practice also diverged – we must not believe that the Church during the Middle Ages totally prohibited people from practicing secular music in their private lives or if it ever wanted to do so. Nevertheless, an immense part of medieval musical life remains largely unknown to us: no one noted, not in the ninth nor even in the fifteenth century, what the peasants sang at work in the fields, what they played during the May dance, what families sang together on winter evenings and what mothers sang to their children at bed time what minstrels presented in the marketplace and what the *Landsknecht* (the "servants of the land") growled in taverns (it was probably unsuitable for minors). This everyday music in the lives of the people in a town and village, which centuries later would be known as "folk songs" and "folk music" and which does not require any theory, we know in the truest sense of the word only from hearsay – it was not written down, nor did any scholars engage in it.

This centuries-long failure to observe everyday music led to philologists to mistake the first written evidence of a form of expression for its actual origin. So, one will occasionally read that the Christmas nativity song "Joseph, lieber Joseph mein," written in the fourteenth century, or "Lullaby" by the English composer William Byrd in 1588, are the first lullabies in music history. If we did not know that mothers sang lullabies, even in parts of the world where there is no Christmas, then this fallacy would be a perfectly credible hypothesis.

Music on Earth

Only in the records of later centuries, with an increasingly literate society, can we find more concrete evidence of music in the everyday life of villages and towns – of course the customs described are usually much older than their first mention. For instance, one reported custom was prevalent in Franconia and Swabia in 1500, but probably goes back further: at the evening round dance in the summer, a mystery would be solved in song in exchange for a symbolic prize from a beautiful girl. Sebastian Franck mentions this "wreath-singing" in his *Weltbuch* in 1534, under the customs of St John's Day, the day of the shortest night:

> The maidens make rose pots on this day, meaning they make pots full of holes; the holes are glued shut with rose petals and

a light is stuck in the holes, just like is done with lanterns, and the pots are then hung are hung out of the window shutter. Also often during summer time, the maidens sing in a circle, the journeymen enter the ring and sing together in a rhyme-like manner. A wreath made of cloves is the prize for whoever performs the best song.[15]

Franck transfers a version of what the men were singing. It is a long exchange with multiple roles. Let us make another stop on our journey and step into a village square on a summer evening in 1497, somewhere between Augsburg and Nuremberg. A singer enters the circle of those gathered, introduces himself as a well-traveled man who knows how to behave, politely greets everyone present and then announces a challenge:

> Is there any singer in this circle who might hear me and whom
>   I don't know?
> He should not deliberate too long and jump in to me quickly.
>
> Singer, now listen to me! I want to pose a question to you:
> What is higher than God and what is bigger than derision
> and what is whiter than the snow, and what is greener than the
>   clover?
>
> If you can sing or tell that to me, you shall win the little wreath;
> therefore I will stand still now and invite the singer to me.

Then another singer enters the stage, and after some formulaic niceties he solves the riddle and asks for the little wreath. However, he immediately places it back into the game by posing a riddle to a girl that has also now stepped into the ring:

> Virgin, tell me in a timely manner, which is the middle bloom in
>   the little wreath?
> There are indeed many flowers around in this little wreath.

The question is asked in this way so that the virgin remains artistically silent, because she herself is the answer to the riddle, the beautiful flower in the middle of the wreath. Therefore, the singer wins the wreath, pays wordy homage once again to the virgin and excuses himself.

Through the transference of songbooks from the sixteenth century, the melody and lyrics of wreath-singing were captured in writing. However, the content of the recorded exchanges and Franck's description of the custom allow us to assume that the men originally sang extemporaneously in competition. The written record merely contains one of many possible versions.

In this tradition, the musical form of which was not just a song but rather a kind of improvised dance-theater, the custom of the evening round dance was merged with the medieval tradition of riddle songs as well as the cross-cultural ritual of the singing dispute. Whether wreath-singing was a learned rural imitation of the art of the Meistersingers or whether the craft preceded this long before, it is difficult to determine.

In the sixteenth century the tradition was prohibited in several places. This indicates that "winning the wreath through singing in the evening also implies a sexual connotation" as Ludwig Uhland remarked in 1866. The wreath is not only a symbol for "laureate," but also of virginity.

However, Martin Luther handled this moral problem with more creativity than the authorities. He simply used a popular melody for a spiritual song and slightly rephrased the text of the first stanza. The secular original goes like this:

> Ich kumm aus frembden landen her
> und bring euch vil der newen mär.
> Der newen mär bring ich so vil,
> mer denn ich euch hier sagen will.

Luther's slightly modified Christmas version is very popular in Germany:

> Vom Himmel hoch, da komm ich her,
> ich bring euch gute neue Mär.
> Der guten Mär bring ich so viel,
> davon ich singen und sagen will.

Also, the poet Hermann Vulpius added to a spiritual song text the remark: "In the tune how one sings for the wreath". This was so well-known that everyone knew without notes how the new spiritual song needed to be sung.

The Invention of the Audience

In the centuries between the Migration Period and the beginning of industrialization, the history of European music shows fulminant changes, aesthetic revolutions and brilliant personalities: Guido of Arezzo, around 1000, the counterpoint of Josquin Desprez around 1500, Monteverdi, the birth of basso continuo and opera around 1600, Johann Sebastian Bach's perfected compositional technique and complex symbolism after 1700, Ludwig van Beethoven and the final independence of artistry around 1800. These are the milestones in the history of composition and musical high art in Europe which music historians are particularly interested in.

However, the music in the lives of the so-called "ordinary people" who lived in the cities and especially in the country, did not fundamentally change over the centuries. Nevertheless, their musical life was infinitely rich, involving many musical occasions, events and ceremonies. National and regional peculiarities shaped these ceremonies over the course of centuries, but the main theme in all evolved peasant cultures, especially under harsh living conditions, was always the strengthening of social community. This theme was expressed particularly in rituals and festivals, where singing, dancing or playing an instrument were never missing.

What changed over the centuries is the relationship between "above" and "below." The Middle Ages lacked the connection between learned high art and the musical practice of the people. Church music was already "esoteric" in the original sense of the word because it was not sung in the national language, but in Latin. Farmers and craftsmen could not participate in the art of the aristocracy. In return, folk culture remained in its own class and, barring a few exceptions, was largely ignored by both the Curch and the aristocracy.

During the period from 1600 to around 1750, which nowadays we call capital B this situation changed. A new middle class had grown, the urban bourgeoisie, where society reinvigorated itself also in musical terms. On the one hand it copied aristocratic lifestyle, and on the other it made down-to-earth traditions socially acceptable. Long-disdained instrumental music gained more prestige. Folk dances, still condemned as impious by Tractate XCVIII in 1954, mingled with the previously purely aristocratic dance societies that conquered the parquet of the bourgeois and aristocratic circles in Europe. In the cities, opera houses were opened that were accessible to all classes.

Notes were widely spread through the printed book and house music became fashionable, spiritual and worldly in style. Boethius' dictum of the precedence of music theory before music practice, which determined the conception of music for centuries, was broken: similar to jazz today, this affective and effective rich, sensual music flourished, especially with the virtuosity of performing musicians. The artist displayed his mastery by versing the musical structure erected by the composer according to the rules of art. And so the stars of stages and concert halls were born.

But it is right here – and here we make another brief musical stop on our journey – where a new division of musical culture took place, a development that had been noted many centuries before, towards the end of classical antiquity, before Plato: the separation of the musical community into a stage and an audience.

Of course, the "passive" audience had come into existence long before. But *concert* means that people gather in one place *because* the music that they want to listen to is performed there. In contrast, music is performed in a church service or at a festival *because* people gather there (primarily because of a different reason). This is a fundamental difference. The more music disengages from the old functional contexts and becomes an end in itself, an item of entertainment, the more a market develops itself for this entertainment, the more professional its providers become. They are met by customers who appreciate the pleasures of art and are willing to pay a price for it – music during the age of radios, CDs and iPods is a commodity that is taken for granted, but in the seventeenth and eighteenth centuries this situation was a novelty and moved society.

In London, thousands of people flocked to the evening garden concerts in the stylishly appointed Vauxhall Gardens, they also did so Frankfurt and Hamburg, where Georg Philipp Telemann established weekly concerts funded by public subscriptions.

At concerts, but especially in opera houses, people weren't always well-mannered. Pop scandals like smashed-up guitars or exposed breasts probably would not have shocked the opera audiences of the early eighteenth century too much. In a satire of Italian opera, the composer Benedetto Marcello describes the following scene:

> After the soprano finishes his part he eats oranges, sniffs and sneezes, and drinks Spanish wine in the public eye, expresses his sympathy to friends and girlfriends in the box seats, teases a

female admirer with fiery declarations of love or sinister threats of revenge, leans in towards the orchestra and explains with a loud voice, while pointing to his throat, that he would have done better if he did not have a bad cold.[16]

The audience wasn't more disciplined:

> In the spacious, well-designed auditorium, good company filled the boxes, while the middle class and commoners sat on benches on the parterre [...]. The noise is predominant. It's understood that some noisy conversation is inevitable before the curtain opens, but here it's something else [...]. Those who are not talking, dedicate themselves are eating on their bench. Everything is allowed: the audience on the ground floor does not waive food and drink, not even [...] after the performance has begun. [...]
>
> One anticipates the aria, the "major piece," which decides each scene according to a procured rite of the opera. But the endless, boring recitatives fill the spaces between the effect pieces. But now the recitatives are not heard by anyone, except a small band of music devotees that follow the score by the light of a candle. However, the rest of the audience remains, in the completely blacked-out room, dedicated to lively conversation [...]. Finally, the aria is conducted; one listens to it devotedly in the sudden onset of silence. The only bad thing is that no one waits for the end of the presentation before applauding with hands and feet and celebrating the singer with shouts of admiration.[17]

Concerts and operas were celebrated events, but did not take on the civil religious rank that listeners ascribed to them 200 years later through their silent devotion. The secular concert and opera music of the eighteenth century, which we include nowadays in the category of "classical" or "serious" music, was in its time modern, popular entertainment for the aristocracy and bourgeoisie. Only church music was "serious." Below "artistic" music was only traditional folk music, which was certainly not spoken of as such.

With concerts a part of everyday life, music education became professionalized. One of the first music conservatories was an orphanage in Venice where none other than Antonio Vivaldi taught gifted girls the violin. However, the acclaimed singing stars of the time were men – castrated men who sang with the voice of a boy. At some point it was discovered that a boy who loses his testicles before puberty and survives this injury retains his high voice. The body keeps on growing after castration, but because the male hormones are missing, the voice does not break.

Castrated men spoke and sang in soprano or alto, but because their chests often became grotesquely large, they had extraordinary breath capacity that gave their boyish voices a large volume and wondrous radiance – provided they had a capable singing teacher.

Hundreds of thousands of children of poor parents between Venice and Palermo were delivered to the "knife" in the hope of a brilliant career. As this practice had actually been banned long ago, some pretended that the boy had been bitten by a wild goose. Many children died because of it, and a nameless majority eked out a miserable existence because they lacked talent. Only a few would achieve fame, questionable compensation for such maltreatment.

Some attribute this bizarre aspect of the Baroque era back to St Paul's verdict that women had to be silent in church and consequently could not sing. However, this relationship with church music is probably only half the truth, as the *evirati* (or *castrati*) enjoyed the greatest success on the opera stage. In the milieu of powdered wigs, the zeitgeist that celebrated the artificial and loved the mannered spectacle, is it surprising that this grotesque distortion of human nature would thrive?

A Song in All Things

The "democratization of music" in Europe continued to progress with the French Revolution, as is said in many music history books. More precisely we mean the "democratization of music listening," meaning the propagation of concert life on audiences from all walks of society. Political transition was also reflected in music styles: the feudal aesthetics of the Baroque became unfashionable in the second half of the eighteenth century. We can recognize the pursuit of true expression - meaning an informal and simple form - in operas by Wolfgang Amadeus Mozart, in Joseph Haydn's oratorio *The Creation*, and in other Viennese classics.

If we consider being musically active in ancient times and church music in the Middle Ages as a central instrument for the education of man, now the concert is viewed as a significant educational institution. Johann Nikolaus Forkel, Johann Sebastian Bach's first biographer wrote in 1780, "After the undeniable decline of church and theater music, musical concerts are the only remaining means by which taste is spread and the higher, final aim of music can be reached."[18]

Since the French Revolution, awareness of civil equality also played a role in the process of music democratization. A musical lexicon from 1802 defines the term "concert" as "fully polyphonic music that is organized for the public so that every lover of the art has the same rights, after paying an entry fee, to participate."[19]

Around mid-1800, influential music critic (a profession that emerged as a byproduct of the invention of the audience) Eduard Hanslick ascribed an intellectual and exclusive understanding of music to the art of the concert hall: "A concert [forms] the principal place of music as such, as a special art. To this extent, self-entitled and independent art of music is only present in the concert hall, everywhere else it only works in conjunction with other arts, as part of a whole or serving external purposes."[20]

Through this inclusion and exclusion, Hanslick, a friend of Brahms and an opponent of Wagner, strengthens the intrinsic value of "absolute" art music. It requires no external purpose (such as liturgy, dance, theater or celebration) for its right to exist, but "forms moved by sound are the sole content and subject matter of music." So, music becomes "musical art," *l'art pour l'art*, of which the highest form is "*absolute pure instrumental music.*"[21]

Hanslick called for a revision of musical aesthetics based solely on the work, the *opus*, excluding the consideration of extramusical content and the psychological effects of music. He therefore goes against what he calls the romantic "feeling of aesthetics." "Music consists of tone rows and tone forms, which have no other content than their own [...]. Even if everyone would regard and name the effect of a tone art by their individuality, the content of the same is precisely none other than the heard tone forms; because music does not only speak through tones, it only speaks tones."[22] Hanslick's views sustainably influenced the intellectual, humanistic concept of music. The reduction of music to the "work," in the form of the score, determines musicology today. It is a bit like if the history of architecture no longer dealt stone palaces and churches but only with their paper construction plans. In general, scholastic analysis of music considers the structure of the score (i.e., the harmony and compositional structure), but disregards to a large extent extra-musical contexts as well as aspects of interpretation (how the score is implemented into the actual performance), which naturally differs depending on the artist and playing tradition.

However, music historiography dedicates itself mainly to the life and works of prominent composers. In the newest edition of the biggest German music lexicon, *Musik in Geschichte und Gegenwart* (Music in history and the present), the article about Wolfgang Amadeus Mozart takes up more than one hundred and fifty small print columns. It is, so to speak, its own biography of Mozart, the size of a book. But composers of medium-level fame have also received detailed contributions. The entry on Giacomo Meyerbeer, for example, consists of 23 columns; the Austrian Carl Ditters von Dittersdorf has at least 19. In contrast, the article about the most famous female opera singer of the twentieth century, Maria Callas, only receives three columns. Also, Dietrich Fischer-Dieskau, who not only has epoch-defining significance as a song interpreter, but who was also busy as a versatile music writer, and the conductor Nikolaus Harnoncourt, *the* pioneer of "historically informed" performances of early music, each receive three columns. Incidentally, the article about the critic Hanslick is a little over five columns.

Until today, the subject of intellectual musical activity was constituted by merging two ideas: the preference of musically skilled writers to performing musicians, formulated by Boethius and reaffirmed in the Middle Ages, and the noble art and craft concept of Hanslick's influence. The score and its creator are the focal point; the actual musical sound is of secondary importance.

However, it is clear how, during a concert, the audience's attention shifts to the performer. Because of the high artistic demand and increasing commercialization of bourgeois concert life, the dazzling Baroque aesthetic of the eccentric viruoso was constant throughout the nineteenth century and shaped the music business to this day. The "Devil's Violinist," Niccolo Paganini, had to repeat an evening concert in Vienna eighteen times, despite the exorbitant ticket prices. The fuss caused by Jenny "The Swedish Nightingale" Lind's 1850 tour was even the subject of newspapers cartoons.

But as fervently enthusiastic as the audience was about the high art of the podium and stage, this unreachable sphere had drifted away from the parquet. It's therefore not surprising that the ever-widening gap between the active artist and the passive music-lover created currents that sought to compensate for it. Art music was no longer just exclusively for the stage, but was more often performed in middle-class living rooms by *dilettanti* – not a derogatory term in the nineteenth century, just the common word for an amateur musician. This was composed art music as opposed to folk music, which had long been the craft of nonprofessional singers and musicians.

A chronicler in Dortmund reported in 1830, "The love of music has spread not only among the affluent middle-class, but also down to the lowest classes so that one can frequently hear some kind of instrument playing from places one would not have expected it to, such as small houses and even huts."[23] This development was at times looked upon condescendingly from an intellectual and academic perspective:

> One can hardly ask now: who is musical? But instead: who is not? In so-called higher or educated circles, music has been an essential part of for long; every family urges it, possibly for all member, without much regard for talent and desire [...]. Even in the circles of retail and trade, during the times of ever pressing shortage of work, money was taken away from the business to at least obtain a piano, music sheets, a teacher and music education for daughters, mainly in the hope that they will be accepted amongst the "well-educated."[24]

However, Robert Schumann allowed his fantasy figure, Florestan, to warn his impressionable alter ego, Eusebius, of an off-art conceit: "Beware though, Eusebius, not to value the dilettantism that is inseparable from artistic life (in a better sense) too low. Because the saying 'Not an artist, not in the loop' must be portrayed as a half-truth as long as one cannot prove a period in which art has flourished without any interaction."[25] The main medium of this interaction was the piano. Around 1800, the *pianoforte* (the name comes from the fact that, unlike the harpsichord, one can play softly or loudly depending on the strength of the stroke) became, thanks to its technical development, the most popular musical instrument in its time, especially in private use. Between 1800 and 1860, over 500 piano factories were established in Germany. According to the findings of a German instrument construction magazine, almost 600,000 pianos were built in Germany from 1850 to 1879;

up until the First World War, it was more than 3 million, slightly more than half of which were exported. Leading Parisian piano-maker company Pleyel is said to have had an annual production of 1,000 instruments as early as 1824.

The grand piano created a focal point for art-loving hostesses, who would invite members of musical society into their homes to listen to virtuosic, sometimes sentimental "salon music." The upright piano (now simply called piano) moved into modest apartments as a piece of furniture.

Both bourgeois house music and elegant salon music were private rather than public areas of musical life. In fact, the interaction that Robert Schumann pointed out took place because art music went from concert halls and theatres into homes and vice versa. Editing and arranging orchestral scores for the piano made it possible to play symphonic works at home. Numerous chamber music pieces were composed and transferred solely for dilettanti. More demanding chamber music, such as string quartets and piano trios, were first played in private circles and eventually found their way into concert halls later in the nineteenth century. In the domestic and social sphere, a lyrical-musical genre developed like no other into quintessential German romantic expression, and is so authentically German that the English and French also use the German term *Lied* when they mean a romantic art song.

We stop the coach again at this point on our journey through musical cultural history and enter the house of Privy Counselor von Staegemann and his wife Elizabeth on Jägerstraße in Berlin-Friedrichstadt, on a Friday night in November of 1816.

As on every Friday, Mrs von Staegemann expects guests because she has been holding a literary-musical salon gathering for years, a casual company of artistically active and interesting people accompanied by tea and pastries. A man in his forties sits at the piano and plays a sonata by Clementi. He is the musician Ludwig Berger, who no longer appears in public as a pianist because he suffers from a nervous disorder in his arm, but who composes and has an excellent reputation as a piano teacher. The doorbell rings and the housemaid leads the guests inside: the painter Wilhelm Hensel, his still very young and pious sister Luise, another young man in an old German costume, and the poet and philology student Wilhelm Müller from Dessau. Ludwig Berger jumps up from the piano and hurries over to Luise, kissing her hand. Müller somewhat mockingly screws up his face and mumbles something, but Mrs von Staegemann immediately strikes up a charming conversation and then has someone call for her daughter Hedwig, a slender 17-year-old with alter eyes and a mischievous smile, who immediately pull Louise to the tea table. A little later, Friedrich Förster, the last guest of the evening, arrives. He is still marked by a serious injury; until recently, he, Müller and Hensel fought as volunteers in the liberation wars against Napoleon.

After several cups of tea, the hostess addresses the round; those present are certainly interested to see if Master Berger had translated into music the poems that Müller and some of the others from the gathering recently submitted to him. "Yes," Muller exclaims excitedly, "now we all want to try this brand new game and enjoy ourselves - or weep hot tears, depending on how it moves us!"

Berger, always slightly introverted, takes some handwritten music sheets from a folder and places them on the piano. Mrs von Staegemann looks around and asks if everyone has chosen their part. Müller (German for miller) says his name already states which role he has. The others laugh approvingly. But he continues: if he could make a wish as to whom should get the role of Rose, the miller's lovely maid… He looks intensely at Luise Hensel. She blushes and quietly says that she's not interested in singing something so coquettish; she'd rather play the gardener, as she had already prepared the verses. "Right, why not a trouser role" says Mrs von Staegemann. "But if none of the young men wants to wear the dress of the miller's fair maid, then this fate will have to fall on her good child." Hedwig's eyes flash and she replies: "Well, the!"

After a playful banter between Hensel and Förster, who are allocated the remaining roles of the hunter and squire, the game begins: Berger accompanies the freshly toned poems on the piano, the others stand or sit in a semicircle around the instrument and sing the songs, more or less from the sheet, according to the assigned roles. Berger has set them as strophic songs in "folk style," which is easy to sing without much effort, even for dilettanti:

Eine Mühle seh' ich blinken
Aus den Erlen heraus,
Durch Rauschen und Singen
Bricht Rädergebraus.

Ei willkommen, ei willkommen,
Süßer Mühlengesang!

Und das Haus, wie so traulich!
Und die Fenster, wie blank!

Und die Sonne, wie helle
Vom Himmel sie scheint!
Ei, Bächlein, liebes Bächlein,
War es also gemeint?

    The poems are half Müller's, and half from other members of the circle. The sequence of songs results in an event in which Rose stands in the center, the "lovely maid of the mill." She is being courted by the squire, the gardener, the hunter and the miller alike. Because she finally decides boldly on the hunter with his green coat, the distraught miller falls into the rushing stream and finds death there. However, perhaps the piece can also end differently – the poet Ludwig Rellstab calls this game "a kind of dramatic task, only solvable through the linking of songs." In this artistically subtle role-playing, the age-old idea of improvised, musical problem-solving shines through, a "psychodrama with music" so to speak, which is in principle not unlike medieval wreath-singing as well as the singing dispute.
    We also know that the abysmal scenario of the "miller's lovely maid" did not lack a real background to the circle of participants. Both Wilhelm Müller and Ludwig Berger, the man at the piano, raved glowingly about a young lady; however, she wasn't the "miller's maid", Hedwig von Staegemann, but Luise Hensel, who belonged to a religious revival movement and turned down all male advances. One should not regard the song cycle as too serious and tragic, but as an ironic play with a folk sentimentality that became fashionable, as can be seen from a prologue that Müller added to the poem's print version some years later:

I invite you, lovely ladies, clever gentlemen,
And all who enjoy a scene well played,
To this, the very latest entertainment,
In the very latest style,
Simply crafted, with no fancy trimmings,
Adorned with noble German skill,
Smart as a young soldier in his best uniform,
And just a little pious – to suit the hearth;

That should suffice to recommend me;
If that is to your taste, then step right in.

Müller's songs didn't become known worldwide in Ludwig Berger's Berlin version, but certainly did with the Viennese Franz Schubert (1797–1828), who some years later composed a song cycle from the poems called *Die schöne Müllerin* (*The Fair Maid of the Mill*). It was Schubert who led the form of the art song "to a never previously seen height."[26] But the song from the nineteenth century was (like its predecessor) in general "not suited to be played in a concert, but was only meant for home musical practice."[27] Max Friedlaender pointed this out decades later, when the pieces of Schubert, Schumann and Brahms had long since conquered the concert hall, and cities like Berlin enjoyed several weekly recitals. However, the songs of Franz Schubert were built around the nucleus of private, convivial friends gatherings in *Schubertiades*. It was here that the court opera singer Johann Michael Vogl sung them when the ink was still wet on the manuscript paper. But at that time the widespread printed song was almost exclusively sung in homes and in music salons, unanimously or polyphonically, by amateurs and the musically versed.

Besides *Die schöne Müllerin*, Schubert transferred another series of poems by Wilhelm Müller to music in *Winterreise* (*Winter Journey*). Schubert composed the song cycle in the last year of his short life. Joseph von Spaun, one of his closest friends, later recalled,

> Schubert was gloomy for some time and seemed to feel beleaguered. When I asked what was going on within him, he replied, "Well, you will soon hear and understand." One day he said to me, "Come to Schober's today, I will sing you a wreath of dreadful songs. I am eager to hear what you will say. They have beleaguered me more than was the case with any other songs." He sang to us now the entire *Winterreise* in a moving voice. We were quite amazed by the gloomy mood of these songs and Schober said that he only liked one song, "Der Lindenbaum" (The Linden Tree). Schubert only said to this, "I like these songs more than all the others and you will like them too."

To call "Der Lindenbaum", which begins with the famous line "Am Brunnen vor dem Tore, da steht ein Lindenbaum" ("By the fountain, near the gate, there stands a linden tree"), a folk song is not quite incorrect,

A Schubertiade (drawing by Moritz von Schwind, 1868). At the piano is Franz Schubert and next to him, leaning back a bit, is the singer Johann Michael Vogl.

though the music was written by Schubert from a poem by Müller. Like no other art song, "Der Lindenbaum" was a work-in-progress that would welcome new developments. It was the Swabian choral pioneer Friedrich Silcher who the first to "transform the song into a folk melody"[28] in 1846, as a set for a four-part male choir.

In this process, Silcher followed a movement century, and also influenced it significantly of interaction between the "above" and "below" of music in the nineteenth century. With new ideals of civil society and national identity – which were, during the times of the governmental dismemberment of the German-speaking area, quite revolutionary – singing societies and clubs were opened throughout the entire nation. In these clubs, sociability played as important a role as the cultivation of music.

Since salons were a female domain and the domestic piano would primarily serve for the musical education of daughters, male choral singing clubs became dominant (and those who still recall Tacitus, the singing clan of the "Wolf People" or the football stadium might not attribute the relationship between male solidarity and singing exclusively to social circumstances). A German Choral Society reached 54,000 members at its first federal festival in Dresden in 1865, and continued to grow steadily. Choral singing became a mass movement.

The repertoire of the choir was "folklorically" shaped to a great extent. Friedrich Silcher also simplified "Der Lindenbaum" into a "folk style" song: he took the melodic theme (which Schubert greatly varied in the strophic) and made a simple strophic song without instrumental accompaniment. Müller's poem contains many subjects that address the subconscious and that we commonly find in folk poetry: love, homecoming, protection, a tree by a fountain where a traveler finds refreshment and rest – but also the reinterpretation of this rest to as rest that lasts forever. "Der Lindenbaum" is an example of an art song that became a folk song. Conversely, orally transmitted poetry and music, of which spiritual and secular high art had hardly taken notice over the centuries, became a subject of artistic and intellectual in the nineteenth century. Poet and philosopher Johann Gottfried Herder had already published a collection of German and foreign poems and songs under the title *Volkslieder (Folk Songs)* in the 1770s. Thus, a key term was born. Through the folk song, Herder wanted to instill in people a human and national (not nationalistic) consciousness, values he saw crystallized in simple folk poetry.

Later, other folk songs collections and musical arrangements followed, such as the English and Scottish folk songs by Joseph Haydn. Shortly after 1800, poets Achim von Arnim and Clemens Brentano released a collection of song texts, which they called *Des Knaben Wunderhorn (The Boy's Magic Horn)*. Although some of these children's songs, love songs and soldier songs are probably the creations of the publishers, the collection increased enthusiasm for folk songs in the following decades and inspired composers such as Schumann, Brahms and Mahler. Thus, a romantic longing for harmony with nature, the scientific motif, a desire to explore cultural roots and the need for artistic representation (which had all disappeared at the beginning of the industrial age) took centre stage.

The interest of romantics in folk music mainly led to the discovery of cultural differences. Art music from the Middle Ages up to Rococo, was European-determined art music, not national or regional. In the sixteenth century, Spaniard Tomas Luis de Victoria composed vocal polyphony in the same style as his Italian and Franco-Flemish colleagues. Those who wrote operas in Europe during the seventeenth century did so in Baroque Italian style. During the eighteenth century, a fugue or a sonata was created according to the same rules in Stockholm, Prague and Rome. Local color was not appropriate (except in dance music), for the musical stratosphere was not permeable enough for influences from the near-bottom class, which of course already differed regionally. Only Romanticism saw that the cultural expressions of the people – of their own and of others – were not inconsequential. "The thought to pave the way for one's own poetry and music to neighboring people," musicologist Kurt Pahlen writes, "reinforces the overall awakening desire to be able to perform one's values and strengths for one's own people. In the large merger between art and folk music, which begins now, folk music is of course the weaker one, but it brings new spirit and new beauty to art music."[29]

Mazurkas and Polonaises found their beginnings in the virtuoso piano music from Frédéric Chopin's home, Schubert composed *Ländler*, and Friedrich Smetana created a large symphonic cycle titled *Má vlast* (*My Country*), musically inspired by the Vltava River. Just as Smetana's music sounds bohemian, the *Peer Gynt* suite by Edvard Grieg evokes Scandinavian landscapes. But the immediate musical expression of people is the song, so it is no coincidence that just as in songs, the layers of art music and popularity must mix and mingle. The song, which arose from everyday life, influences life and society and yet is maintained, defaced, refined and hacked up, but hardly ever completely forgotten.

Schubert's "Der Lindenbaum" continues to influence. Silcher's process was the starting point for further choral arrangements and monophonic melodic editions of the song, which moved away from the "original." This is how an art song actually transforms into a folk song – which is, strictly defined, a song handed down orally, whose composer and poet are not known.

In Thomas Mann's novel *Der Zauberberg*, young Hans Castorp is lost listening to a gramophone playing Schubert's "Lindenbaum". When the outbreak of the First World War wakes him like a thunderbolt from his seven-year dream in the sanatorium, Hans, with "Der Lindenbaum" on his lips, voluntarily enters the war as Wilhelm Müller once did, though his return is uncertain.

At the end of the second disaster of the twentieth century, in March of 1945, amid the rubble of Berlin, singer Peter Anders and pianist Michael Raucheisen meet in the broadcasting building of the Reich.

They have dedicated themselves to the seemingly unworldly task of rehearsing Schubert's entire *Winterreise*. Despite the new recording technology of the Magnetophon reel-to-reel, each of the 24 songs is produced without cuts, because time is of the essence: the Red Army is only 60 kilometers away.

Thirteen years later, the world seems to be safe and sound again and a maudlin Rudolf Schock sings the song with a children's choir in the movie *Das Dreimäderlhaus (House of the three girls)*, a fictionalized account of Schubert's life. The film is based on the highly successful operetta of the same name, written by Henrich Berte at the beginning of the twentieth century using Schubert's music.

Today, on YouTube, the most viewed recordings of "Am Brunnen vor dem Tore" belong to the "modern" adaptations of Nana Mouskouri and Helmut Lotti. This is the direction the "Lindenbaum" is taking us (and likewise, the direction in which we are taking the song) – right into the twentieth century with all its cuts, breaks and radical changes.

Highlights of Modern Times

Music history lists numerous innovations and artistic revolutions since Franz Schubert's time. However, good books about music history already exist in abundance; the focus of this book is a different one. Some questions are visible as a red thread in the "cultural history" section: Which functions does music fulfill over time? What significance does society allocate to music. What do people mean by the word "music" – an art form, a means to an end, a commodity? What remains of the "original" contexts of the communication and the bond in which our musical behavior has developed itself? How do culture and civilization change the concept of music? Who plays music, for what, who listens to it, when and where, and how does the player relate to the listener?

The developments of the musical life in the Western world accelerated and rushed through the twentieth century. The situation in modern times appears complex and confusing. However, there are a few milestones and course settings that have given the concept and handling of music particularly sustainable and radical turns. Therefore, we initially consider only two highlights that will bring our musical journey to its penultimate stop on our way to the present – and later we'll think about what these seemingly unrelated observations have to do with each other and what they mean in our current musical life.

The 22nd December 1877 edition of the New York magazine *Scientific America* reported, "Mr. Thomas A. Edison recently came into this office, placed a little machine on our desk, turned a crank, and the machine inquired as to our health, asked how we liked the phonograph, informed us that it was very well, and bid us a cordial good night."[30] Edison's invention will continue to radically change the understanding of music, just like the development of musical notation did approximately 1,000 years ago. A songbook and an orchestral score record the blueprints of music, but music can only sound during the moment of its performance, *in statu nascendi*. Thus all music is an event of the moment, fleeting, unrepeatable and unique; the same piece is always a new creation with each performance, even if only in the minutest details.

The phonograph stores the vibrations of sound in a groove on tin foil or a wax roll, transferred via a needle. The same needle then makes them audible again. This technique could seem rather inadequate when compared with later developments in electrical and digital sound recording, but it represented a fundamental step: an acoustic event can be preserved and repeated as often as wanted. The listener, who could previously only listen to music *live* where it was being played (in a concert hall, theater or private performance), can do this now in any place at any time, separately from the performers and not necessarily in company – thus far a must for all music.

The music industry developed rapidly in the following years: at the turn of the century in Hanover, up to 10,000 records were pressed from shellac every day. About ten years later, complete recordings of symphonies and even operas were already commercially available. With a playing time of five minutes on one side of a shellac record, the music-lover who wanted to hear a symphony would have to turn over and switch records several times, as well wind up the spring mechanism of the gramophone with a crank. Regardless, the record had become a mass medium at the beginning of the twentieth century.

"There is probably no opera of the twentieth century that touched the hearts of a wide audience as dearly as *Der Rosenkavalier*," Kurt Pahlen writes about the opera by Richard Strauss, which premiered in 1911. That's saying something, because so-called serious music ran into limitations at the beginning of the twentieth century. Even Richard Wagner, in his opera *Tristan und Isolde* from 1865, was already handling harmonic language so that it no longer resolved dissonant chords: the tension, the desire for resolution becomes almost unbearable.

Richard Strauss asked even more from his audience in Dresden in 1909. With the mythological *Elektra*, Strauss sets a tragedy of terrible proportions to music. Vindictiveness and frantic desperation express themselves in an orchestral tumult and seem to lose all connection to the tonic, the basic note. Only when Elektra sees her presumed dead brother Orestes again does the atonality dissolve temporarily into streaming major harmonies. Strauss admits himself that he went "to the extreme limits of harmony, psychological polyphony [...] and the perceiving capacity of today's ears in this opera."

What can follow that? For Strauss the answer was a step back. He had defeated boundaries and let the charm and abuse of the Rococo period bloom again in English translation? in accompaniment to the ingenious and witty libretto by Hugo von Hofmannsthal, in which the musical language of the *fin-de-siècle* is of course voluptuous and bold, but interwoven with the blessedness of the Viennese waltz and repeatedly striking tonal roots. Sometimes *Der Rosenkavalier* is characterized as a "farewell to the sinking Austro-Hungarian Monarchy" and perhaps the entire oeuvre of Strauss, who composed the gorgeous, late-romantic pieces *Vier letzte Lieder* after the Second World War, in the last year of his life, is a farewell to the history of Western music.

The way of the other composers from this time does not only completely detach itself from the roots of music history, but also from the psychology of musical perception. The Viennese Arnold Schoenberg, ten years younger than Strauss, composed six short piano pieces around the same time as *Der Rosenkavalier*. Friedrich Herzfeld judged harshly: "Only shreds of sound blow over to us, there is no recognizable theme, which is why no more motivic work exists. There are unicellular organisms, so to speak."[31]

With these pieces Schoenberg actually set the foundation for a completely new, antitraditional compositional technique that was widely determinative for the musical avant-garde: from the twelve tones of the chromatic scale (i.e., the white and black piano keys in an octave) a row is created not due to a melodic idea, but according to the principle that every tone occurs once within it – kind of like a musical Sudoku. Because the rows and harmonies are not based on a basic tone, consonance and dissonance play a minor part. "The dodecaphony [twelve-tone technique] stems from the head, not from the heart: consequently it can only address the listener's logic, not his emotion," according to Kurt Pahlen. Schoenberg believed in a musical revolution and relied on the willingness of the listener to embrace progression. Initially, there was excitement, which settled after some time – but not because the audience had embraced the new music, but because it had turned away disinterested, preferring either the music of past centuries or a completely different type of "modern" music.

A singing lesson at a university: for the student who is taking singing lessons as part of her studies to become a primary school teacher, it's her first hour. The singing teacher discusses with her which piece they want to tackle first.

> Teacher: I'll give you two pieces that you can peruse a little until next time.
> Student: Great, I'm happy to do it.
> T: Look, this is a small etude by an Italian named Vaccai. It's not difficult. He lived around the same time as Rossini. And then we could also try this song by Mendelssohn.
> S: Yes, well, thank you… One question: could we also sing something modern?
> T: Something modern? Basically yes, but… Modern pieces aren't often easy to begin with!
> S: Oh, alright… But I think I can easily do more with it than the older stuff.
> T: Well, let me see what I can find. How about Britten? Or maybe Weill?
> S: I don't know those two.
> T: Do you have a suggestion?
> S: I brought something along (she takes a sheet from her bag and hands it to the singing teacher).
> T: Ah. "Don't Cry for Me, Argentina." This is more like pop music.
> S: From Madonna!
> T: Okay, let's give it a try! Do you just want to sing it immediately?
> S: I'll try it. (The teacher plays a few beats on the piano and gives the student an opening.)

S: (Singing with a lot of breath in her voice) It won't be easy; you'll think it strange…
T: Yes, well. Just try the following: breathe at the beginning deep down in the belly and open the jaw just a bit, even before the first note! And then you let the sound come (she sings the phrase once for her).
S: Okay, one question: should I sing like you, or rather… normally?
T: What do you mean by "normally?"
S: Well, I would sing it in a more modern style (she sings the first notes again).
T: I see. You mean with a "pop" voice?
S: Madonna also sings it normally.
T: The way you sung it just now there was a lot of breath in your voice. This means that the vocal cords don't close completely and more air than sound comes out. If you wanted to sing something to your class while playing the piano it would be difficult. They would hardly hear you.
S: But Madonna and singers like that have very strong voices!
T: They have a microphone! Without amplification you wouldn't hear much.
S: Really? OK then, may I try again?
T: But of course!

III. Music and Person

Espressivo

Goosebumps, Antibodies and Endorphins

When Frank Schneider comes home from work in the late afternoon he likes to relax with some tea and music. Frank lives alone and owns an extensive collection of CDs, mostly classical and jazz. Today he pulls a recording of the Piano Concerto no. 23 in A Major by Wolfgang Amadeus Mozart from the shelf, puts it into the CD player, sits on his bed and pours himself a cup of tea. The high-quality speakers of his hi-fi system fill the living room with the first lively score of the concerto and soon the tension of the workday drifts away. The cheerful mood of the *allegro* transfers over to him while he leafs through a car magazine. "I'll take the new BMW 3 Series for a test drive," he decides.

After a few minutes the first score is finished and after a brief pause the piano plays without orchestral accompaniment: a delicate, lingering, wistful minor theme in 6/8 time. Frank lowers the magazine and gazes thoughtfully out the window at the cloudy, gray sky. The introduction of the piano is coming to an end as the final chord in F-sharp minor is caught by the lower tone string players, while high above a clarinet sounds with the new, plaintive main theme. Goosebumps erupt on Frank's neck, a comforting nostalgic shiver that runs down his back and spreads to his arms and thighs. After a few seconds it's over. He has listened to the Piano Concerto no. 23 often and knows by now that at this point in the *adagio*, when the orchestra begins, he always gets goosebumps – if it's a good recording. This happens once more as the passage repeats itself.

In the third and final score, a cheerful *allegro assai*, Mozart must share Frank's attention with the car magazine again. After the end of the final score and three cups of tea, feeling refreshed, Frank runs some errands before he heads out on a dinner date.

The phenomenon of goosebumps while listening to music seems to be deeply rooted in our biology. Since time immemorial, music has moved our emotions. In the 1990s, the relatively young neuroscience became increasingly interested in music perception and it is in this field that the phenomenon of physical reactions to music has been investigated in recent years by several researchers.[1] The psychologist Jaak Panksepp reports that many people experience shivers or goosebumps when they hear pieces that touch them emotionally; he names in particular songs that deal with unrequited love and longing, but also music in which patriotic pride and remembrance of fallen warriors is expressed.

Most studies show that not everyone gets goosebumps listening to the same music, but there are certain musical stimuli that will typically have this effect: an unexpected harmonic twist, a crescendo or the contrast between a solo and orchestra or choir. Sad pieces cause shivers more often than cheerful ones, and the reaction is more likely to happen during a piece of music with which one already has a relationship than a piece that is heard for the first time.

A research group led by Eckart Altenmüller at the Hannover University of Music performed a series of spine-tingling experiments in a laboratory. Thirty-eight men and women listened – individually and while being spatially separated from the examiner – to different pieces of music, from Bach to death metal, while they sat in a comfortable armchair and pressed a button as soon as they had goosebumps. It turned out that only twenty-one of the thirty-eight subjects even experienced goosebumps during any of the pieces. Among these twenty-one were musicians and non-musicians just as there were both musicians and non-musicians in the group of seventeen people that didn't feel a shiver run down their back. The reaction has therefore nothing to do with musical experience. It much rather depends on personality type, as psychological tests have proven. Adventurous people that are looking for a "kick" are not prone to goosebumps, whereas those that are feel subtle stimuli intensely. But what even leads to this skin reaction?

The skin of humans, just like that of all mammals, is hairy. At the root of each hair of our body is a tiny, obliquely attached muscle, the *arrector pili*. When these muscles contract the hairs stand up and create small bumps on the skin's surface. As a reaction to cold, this mechanism is easily explainable as a remnant from the time of our ancestors who still wore a thick bodily coat. When they ruffled up their hair it insulated the skin against heat loss.

A contradiction to this hypothesis is that we perceive musical stimuli that cause goosebumps as pleasant. In addition, brain activity during music-induced shivers has been visualized with imaging techniques. This shows a pattern typical of euphoria and other pleasant feelings.

I therefore suspect a slightly different phylogenetic origin of this phenomenon. Heat regulation is not the only biological reason for hair ruffling. There is another function, a signal to the outside: when animals defend themselves or act aggressively, they make themselves look bigger. This is aided visually when an animal ruffles up its coat and thus increases the silhouette of his body: a bluff, if you will. The phrase "My neck hairs are standing on end" reveals that even with us humans our coat still ruffles when we are aggressive or defensively ready. In connection to this, Irenäus Eibl-Eibesfeldt points to the "shiver of emotion" that people experience when their collective readiness for defense is addressed at formal group events such as singing the national anthem. This in turn is consistent with Panksepp's observation of musical situations that cause goosebumps.

But what has the orchestra at the beginning of the *adagio* of Mozart's Piano Concerto no. 23 to do with it? More than it seems at first glance. At this point the composition creates a musically tense relationship between the individual (the piano, which is initially all alone) and the group (the orchestra). The loner suddenly faces the group or is protectively adopted by it. The group surprises with its expansiveness and diversity, the sound spectrum suddenly fans out between the deep basses and high woodwind instruments. The sensation that affects the listener when he participates in this scene is in a literal sense more emotion than a lonely chill, but perhaps it's both. After all, wordless music does not transmit explicit, unambiguous information, it's ambivalent.

Another famous shiver-inducing moment of music is the short performance of the choir in St Matthew's Passion by Johann Sebastian Bach. Pontius Pilate confronts the people (represented by the choir) with a choice: releasing either Barabbas or Jesus. The choir shouts in a dissonant, bloodcurdling chord, "Barabbas!" and thus confronts the listener with a focused aggression against Christ. It's not unreasonable to assume that devout Protestant Bach wanted to bring the listener into an emotional readiness for defense – and he has succeeded.

The shiver that music causes to run down the back is a strong emotional response, one of many different emotional reactions that we can experience through music. The goosebumps example shows that the effect that music has on the listener makes the listener aware of the fact that he is actvely involved in the event. If we currently know more about emotional responses when *listening* to music than emotional responses when *making* music, it's because we can examine a jazz singer in action.

The physical effects of music – when singing and making music as well as listening to it – are of course not limited to goosebumps alone, but affect the entire organism. Music literally goes "under the skin." Every person who plays a musical instrument, sings in a choir, dances or simply listens to music knows this and feels the deep effects. Nevertheless, it is not easy to make scientifically tangible statements about this topic. Science looks for results that are true in general, not only in some cases. In medicine, a drug that helps some people in certain situations would not be worth very much. It is somewhat similar with the physiological effects of music: these depend not only on the type of music and its "form of administration," but also on the situation and of the subject listening or performing music.

From the perspective of human ethology (which was discussed in detail in the first chapter of the book) this is not surprising, because different forms of music are by nature of different behavioral contexts – and that also means physiological relationships are involved.

However, some indications of how music affects the organism can be identified over and over again and they are sometimes quite amazing. It starts in the womb: when a fetus is twenty-two weeks old its inner ear, auditory nerve and brain have developed so that it can perceive sound signals. However, sounds coming from outside are strongly muffled by the abdominal wall and amniotic fluid of the mother before they penetrate the ear of the unborn baby. Nevertheless, we can detect that the heartbeat and movements of the child change with acoustic stimuli. The fetus can clearly distinguish male from female voices, high from low tones and fast melodies from slow ones. Since the mother's voice reaches the baby the best via the bones (which conduct sound), it becomes familiar with the maternal tone of voice before birth – probably even with the songs she sings during pregnancy – and recognizes the familiar sound/voice after birth. However, whether the baby's memory lasts longer than a few weeks or months is controversial.[2]

The importance of lullabies has already been mentioned from an evolutionary perspective. In fact, a clinical study also shows that they have a favorable effect on the development of the child. The song "Guten Abend, gut' Nacht" was regularly sung to twenty of the forty premature infants at a neonatal unit, the other twenty instead received different nonmusical attention. The lullaby babies, both boys and girls, gained weight faster than the babies in the control group.[3]

So, should it become common practice to serenade each newborn several times a day with Brahms's "Guten Abend, gut' Nacht" from a

CD? This question can be negated because the most important aspect when it comes to a lullaby is the personal communication between the caregiver and the child. In contrast to a CD player, the mother, the father or the nurse can respond to the child's reaction.

Canadian psychologist Sandra Trehub, who has dealt for decades with the music perception of small children, discovered that when mothers and fathers sing a song to their child it sounds different than when they sing the same song in the absence of the child. Independent subjects were able to distinguish between recordings with and without the baby's presence. Not only is tempo and pitch different, the emotional expression of the voice also changes involuntarily in the presence of the child: a compelling example of the power of singing as a direct bond between people.[4]

But even "canned" music can sometimes have amazing effects on the human organism. The physician and musicologist Claudius Conrad examined the effect of Mozart's piano music on critically ill patients in Munich, who were in the ICU following surgery and had to be placed on artificial respiration. In order to endure the constant stress of the breathing tube, infusion and postoperative pain, these patients usually need to be sedated with a tranquilizer. Some of the patients were slowly introduced to piano sonatas by Mozart via headphones. The results were that the patients relaxed, their bodies clearly distributed a significantly lower amount of the stress-messenger interleukin 6, and their heart rate and blood pressure declined so much that doctors could go without administering an intravenous sedative during and half an hour after the music playback.

The influence of musical stimuli on heart rate has also been observed in numerous other studies. In 1927, American scientists discovered that the performance theme of the bullfighter Escamillo from Bizet's opera *Carmen* accelerates the heartbeat; however, the beginning of Symphony no. 6 by Tchaikovsky slows the heart rate. Physical reaction apparently depends on the rhythmic and melodic expression of a piece.

The same applies to the impulse to physically move to music. You could say that the rhythm of some dance music "makes you move." We can observe in all possible situations how people snap their fingers or tap their feet to the tempo of music playing in the background. Acoustic signals – apparently more so than visual signals – excite the motor nerve system and place it in a higher state of readiness.

The ability to activate an "internal metronome" and to synchronize body movements to a regular beat is a basic element of human musicality. However, the neurophysiological mechanism will not be explored in detail here.

Another finding of science relates to an interesting connection between music and movement perception. Very loud music with very high intensities in the low frequency range (for example, in a nightclub or at a rave) stimulates, according to studies by Neil Todd and Frederic Cody, not only the hearing organ in the inner ear, but also the organ of balance that is located in the middle ear, and thereby produces full-motion sensations similar to when swinging or riding a roller coaster. This explains why people cover their ears at loud, screeching machine noises, but voluntarily listen to and enjoy loud disco or techno music with booming bass. (Of course social bonding and group experience also play a role.)

Neurobiologist Walter Freeman proposed an interesting hypothesis in this context. The hormone that is secreted both during the female orgasm and the birthing process, and which promotes both the emotional relationship to the sexual partner as well as to the newborn baby, is oxytocin. This hormone might also be released by rhythmic body movements to loud dance music and in trance states; it provides pleasant sensations and could represent a physiological factor of the emotional bond that generates musical group activity.

The question of whether a trance can be initiated immediately by a rapid sequence of deep drum beat frequencies, which has already been discussed in the 1960s (back then it was not directed at discos or raves, but at religious rites of traditional cultures), is controversial. Nevertheless, the enticing effects of loud music can't change the fact that prolonged exposure to sound levels greater than 85 dB(A) will irreversibly damage the fine hair cells in the inner ear. The result is hearing loss. Therefore, labor protection laws in EU member countries require people to wear hearing protection in workplaces where the sound exceeds 80 dB(A). At music events the level is often in the range of 100 dB(A) and above. Gunter Kreutz and his staff at the Department of Music Education at the University of Frankfurt have examined physiological effects of another kind. The results of the study were good for a few headlines in the media – that does not often happen in music pedagogy. Thirty-one singers of an amateur choir gave saliva samples just before and after a rehearsal of Mozart's *Requiem*, from which the scientists were able to determine the concentration of immunoglobulin A (IgA) antibodies. These antibodies protect the upper respiratory passages from infection.

The study revealed that the concentration of IgA in their saliva increased significantly during rehearsal, at the same time improving the subjective mood of the choir. In comparison, Kreutz also determined the IgA concentration before and after listening to a recording of the same piece. Here, the physiological effect did not occur. The physical immune system was only activated through singing, not by merely listening to the music.[5]

The measurable effects of singing, music making and listening to music on human and animal organisms are something of a scientific nucleus in a large complex of folk wisdom about the power of music. The effect of music on animals and even inanimate matter is discussed repeatedly. The language sometimes suggests that witchcraft must have something to do with it. In the second Merseburg Incantation from pre-Christian times, there is talk of healing a horse's sprained leg through singing. Even the Latin word *incantare* (to charm, to bewitch) is derived from *cantare* (to sing). In the Italian language magic is still called *incanto* and the Frenchman gallantly expresses his delight over a new acquaintance with "Enchanté, Madame."

The idea of the physical force of tones is not only reflected in the ethos of the ancient civilizations of Greece and the Orient, but also in myth. The singer Orpheus, who is from the musical people of the Thracians, received the lyre from Apollo. He not only charmed people with his song and lyre, but even animals. Furthermore, Roman Horace rhymes that Orpheus even stopped winds and rivers in their tracks and that oak trees followed his singing.

The largest part of the saga deals with love and loss. When Orpheus' wife Eurydice dies from a snake bite, the mourner is able to soften the lord of the shadow realm with his singing and moves him to give Eurydice back – but on the condition that he does not turn around and look at her. However, the magic singer is overcome by his own excessive emotional involvement and ultimately loses his beloved wife and the transcendent power.

The dramatist Euripides endows Orpheus with the ability to move stones with his music, so that they come harmoniously together to create a structure. We can recognize the counterpart to this story in the biblical account of the destruction of the walls of Jericho. Joshua circles the city several times with the people of Israel; seven priests blow seven trumpets until the city walls finally crumble and the way for the conquest and destruction of Jericho opens. The report of the effect of the trumpets of Jericho – actually an oriental *shofar*, an instrument made from a ram's horn – demonstrates a unique ambivalence of musical power, which is recognized at times as being constructive, other times as destructive, as enchanting as it is disastrous.

The physical experience of a painfully loud whistle or the bodily vibration that is generated by deep booming instruments most likely worked just as well in music mythology as the emotional shiver triggered by a choir or a harmonically rich, clear solo voice that captivates your senses and lets you forget the world around you for a little while. And no one seems immune to it. The companions of Odysseus had to tie the well-traveled hero to the mast of his ship and plug their and his ears with wax, so as not to succumb to the fatal spell of the Sirens, who sit on their rocky island and drive skippers out of their minds with their sweet, intoxicating vocals. Beautiful Lorelei does the same high up on a rock above the Rhine.

In Mozart's famous opera The Magic Flute, Tamino and Papageno receive powerful magical musical instruments, a flute and a glockenspiel, to support their dangerous search for the missing Pamina: "The magic flute will protect you, support you in greatest misfortune. With this you can act almighty, transform the human passions."

By playing the magic flute and little bells, enemies involuntarily begin to sing and dance; even wild animals become tame. Orpheus' motif is given a slightly different shading in *The Magic Flute*, since the three ladies who present the magic instruments are in the service of the evil Queen of the Night. The misuse of musical magic is also a subject in the legend of the mysterious Pied Piper of Hamelin, who with his flute lures away not only rats, but also children. The fascination with the beguiling magic of sound and the fear of its unpredictable power are therefore tied close together.

Today, the fascination with the power of music still remains. The movie *The Story of the Weeping Camel*, produced in 2003 under the direction of the Mongolian film school graduate Byambasuren Davaa and the Italian Luigi Falorni, became a worldwide success. The semidocumentary film tells of a camel who gives birth to a colt in the Gobi Desert but doesn't accept it because she is too weak to nurse the calf. The small camel is close to dying, when the Mongolian pastoral nomads remember an old ritual: a musician from a distant city should make the mother camel weep with the sounds of his horse-head fiddle and soften her heart. In fact, the miracle works: the mother begins to cry, the colt is allowed to drink and is saved.

The plot of the film is fictional but its core motif has a factual background. Many cultures, especially pastoralists, naturally know the musical mating calls for cattle. In Sweden and Norway, shepherdesses use a high, overtone-rich style of singing, the *kulning*, to summon grazing cows, sheep and goats on mountain pastures. Swiss dairymen lure their cows with a sung cattle call for milking, the so-called *Kuhreihen*. Similar traditions are handed down throughout the entire Alp region. Sung cattle calls are an archaic and so far scarcely systematically explored element of regional folk music.

Some stories about the effect of musical stimuli on animals have become very popular through media reports and yet still belong to the realm of fantasy. With the support of the British dairy industry, psychologists Adrian North and Liam MacKenzie from the University of Leicester performed a large study in the 1990s in which they sonicated approximately 1,000 English cows with music for nine weeks. Apparently quiet music, like Beethoven's *Pastoral Symphony*, led to each animal producing an average of 0.73 liters more milk per day. However, with "Back in the USSR" from the Beatles, their udders didn't fill out that much. Even Germany's dairy industry association of North Rhine-Westphalia found similar results in their own study conducted in 1998.

Nevertheless, the measured differences are statistically not significant. Eckart Altenmüller, professor of music physiology and musicians medicine at the University of Music in Hannover, sees the explanation for the effect not in cows, but in humans: "It has been determined that it is not the cows, but that the milker just milked better with music."

Music and Healing

The first book of Samuel in the Old Testament tells of Saul, the first king of Israel, and of his conflict with the seer Samuel. "An evil spirit from the Lord tormented him," it says in Chapter 16. Saul calls his servants and speaks to them:

> So Saul said to his attendants, "Find someone who plays well and bring him to me." One of the servants answered, "I have seen a son of Jesse of Bethlehem who knows how to play the lyre. He is a

brave man and a warrior. He speaks well and is a fine-looking man. And the Lord is with him." Then Saul sent messengers to Jesse and said, "Send me your son David, who is with the sheep." So Jesse took a donkey loaded with bread, a skin of wine and a young goat and sent them with his son David to Saul. David came to Saul and entered his service. Saul liked him very much, and David became one of his armor-bearers. Then Saul sent word to Jesse, saying, "Allow David to remain in my service, for I am pleased with him." Whenever the spirit from God came on Saul, David would take up his lyre and play. Then relief would come to Saul; he would feel better, and the evil spirit would leave him.[6]

This story is probably the original model of a therapeutic approach that we now call *receptive music therapy*. This umbrella term includes those forms of therapy in which the patient listens to music but doesn't make music himself. The idea is based on the comprehensible everyday experience that music can change the mood of the listener, that people react emotionally and sometimes physically to the music they listen to. The concept of receptive music therapy may also be based on the speculative assumption of a comprehensive order, which can, where it is disturbed, be restored by harmonically structured music. However, Pythagoreans and Platonists understood music as something that needs to be learned and practiced, not only listened to.

Henri Matisse, *La Tristesse du Roi* (1952):
David plays for the melancholy King Saul.

Receptive music therapy is, as far as we know, the oldest form of music therapy. Even chanted spells and shamanic rituals are, in a broad sense, receptive music therapy. That is where music experience compresses – as in the Orpheus myth – into an idea of the magical powers of the sung word in the context of a ritual. We recall: vocally ritualized speech is used in exceptional situations.

Even in early modern times, music was administered as a "drug." The polymath Athanasius Kircher wrote in the seventeenth century, "Music opens the air holes of the body from which evil spirits can come forth." The theoretical basis of musical medication shifted slowly from a magical or cosmological worldview towards mechanistic ideas, which of course were still highly speculative in the days when people still believed in the ancient principle of the interaction of good and bad humors or even newer fashions such as the healing power of magnetism.

This is one reason why the scientifically enlightened twentieth century was skeptical about receptive music therapy. The unique effects of listening to music could rarely be empirically detected. Therefore, this therapeutic approach played only a minor role for a long time, until the specific physiological effects of music were examined in more detail in the wake of growing interest in neuroscience in the late twentieth century. Since then, the use of selective forms of receptive music therapy has increased.

Receptive music therapy in the clinical medical field has already been mentioned: musical stimulation of preterm infants or disabled children is supposed to positively influence their development especially in the context of immediate human attention. It is also scientifically proven that one can reduce anxiety in the doctor's office or in the operating room by playing music; it supports the anesthesia and calms the patient during or after medical procedures.

Here, it is debatable whether the patient's favorite music should be played in the treatment room or pieces that generally have a soothing effect due to their musical structure. A study by music psychologist Wolfram Goertz on cardiac catheterization patients shows, similarly to the project by Claudius Conrad, success with the use of Mozart and Bach – even in those patients that usually prefer to listen to hard rock.

Even with tinnitus, the agonizing in-ear noise that permanently affects many people today, receptive music therapy shows remarkable success. Only recently, a working group at the University of Münster has developed a promising method: on a trial basis, patients listened for twelve months to their favorite pieces of music from which the tinnitus frequencies were electronically removed beforehand. The subjective loudness of the ear's noise was reduced under these conditions.[7] The proven effects of "acoustic drug" music, which go beyond subjective improvement of mood, are not numerous but medically significant. The results of corresponding scientific studies should establish medical indication-specific music therapy treatments – because the side effects of drug music are safe. On the other hand, one must recognize that the possibilities of receptive therapy, in which musical stimuli are successfully used as a remedy, have obvious limits: music supposed to fulfill an extra-musical function (and not in the sense of Hanslick, as an absolute art for art's sake), is not an object, it is communication. Music-therapeutical approaches, which are aimed at changing behavior and communication, must therefore contain musical action and not just passive listening. Thus, music psychologists Herbert Bruhn and Eva-Maria Frank-Bleckwedel have formulated an idea that establishes the precedence of *active* over *receptive* music therapy, as follows: "Actually, the influence of music is only created when people handle music: music does not work simply by being present, but only when a client seeks music, listens to it or even actively improvises it. Thus, the term music forms a class of specific behaviors."[8]

Modern music therapy, which became established in Europe in the 1970s, is based on this concept, primarily understood as active music therapy and primarily aimed at "retuning" behavior and psyche. The client uses musical instruments, his voice or his body to express himself musically.

In music therapy practice, both individual therapy as well as group therapy is common. A session can begin with an orientation phase in which the clients – often children, but also adults – explore and try out various musical instruments that are available in the treatment room. In general, these are not violins or transverse flutes, the handling of which requires extensive practice, but instruments that allow sounds to be created without prior knowledge, so that free improvisation is possible: various types of drums, xylophones (as they are also used in Orff-Schulwerk teachings) and other percussive instruments, simple string instruments, pianos or keyboards.

During a music therapy session communication through audition, replay, questions, answers and competition between members of the group or between therapist and client, should be (ideally) created.

Words can often be completely dispensed with, which is important, for example, in working with speech-impaired or autistic people.

The key to music therapeutic coexistence is improvisation, either free or according to rules set by the therapist. Music therapist Tonius Timmermann explains the psychological thought behind it: "Improvising requires having the courage to engage in a game where the next note is always unknown. On a psychological level, most people have to overcome great fear: the unknown and uncontrollable could take them beyond their familiar world in which they feel at home – even if it is a source of suffering."[9] Improvisational play with a musical instrument allows clients to learn and test behaviors that they might not be able to implement in their daily lives or dare not to: a "trial action" as Timmermann puts it.

Music therapists nowadays work in various clinical and social institutions. In psychiatric hospitals they work with people who are suffering from depression or anxiety disorders, but also with addicts and young people who suffer from eating disorders. Music therapists improvise with disabled people, support the healing process of patients in sanatoriums and rehabilitation clinics and stimulate the lost memories of elderly people in nursing homes (we talked at the beginning of the book about Mrs K. and the gramophone). Music therapy can also take place in outpatient practices; it's not unusual for parents of children with behavioral problems to make use of this help. Despite the high degree of institutional integration, health insurance policies don't usually pay for music therapy treatment. Insurance coverage might be taken into consideration in cases involving disabled patients.

Music therapy is defined, according to a policy statement of the Deutsche Musiktherapeutische Gesellschaft (German Music Therapy Society), "by its very nature as psychotherapeutic." It continues, "Music therapeutic methods follow equally deep psychological, behavioral therapeutic learning theory, systemic, anthroposophical and humanistic concepts."[10]

This theoretical and methodological positioning is crucial to understanding the approach: unlike the philosophy of ancient Greece, the main direction of modern music therapy no longer believes "that a relationship between musical phenomena and physiological and psychological processes in man exist, and that music acts specifically on the thinking, feeling will of people through its melodic, harmonic and rhythmic peculiarities. The effect of music unfolds instead as part of a (common) musical activity within a therapeutic relationship."[11]

If in today's German-speaking region established active music therapy is essentially "psychotherapy with music," then that's mainly because of the scientifically justified rejection of the older ideas that sound has a healing effect. The fact that music therapy developed this way during the 1970s and was not "reinvented," that it emanated from Sigmund Freud's and C.G. Jung's methods of psychotherapy (which many pioneers of music therapy have adopted), is also related to the fact that psychoanalysis and psychotherapy were already established concepts in health care. It is probably also no coincidence that the therapeutic qualities of simple musical improvisation have only been discovered in the age of multimedia entertainment and information. A century earlier, singing and music-making was thought of as too common to hold the key to lost wholeness.

Music as "a class of specific behavior types," as opposed to object of art, the recognition of its communicative function and its role in the development of the person – these paradigms of music therapy are consistent in principle with the image of the nature of music as perceived by human ethology. Noteworthy in this context are also the observations on the relationship of traditional (and musical) rituals with modern therapy concepts. This is how some ethnologists have come to recognize situational and functional similarities between the vocal dispute of the Greenland Inuit and European psychotherapy: in both situations the participants face a problem that prevents them from fulfilling their normal function in the community. Social conventions prohibit these facts from being openly presented or acted upon. Thus, a situation is created that is outside the context of everyday life and permits a ruthless handling of the problem.[12]

However, what today's established music therapy (as well as other psychotherapeutic methods) sometimes lacks, is a reliable foundation in theory and studies of efficacy. Presumably, the pressure for fundamental research is remote because there is a great willingness in the population – as music psychologist Klaus Ernst Behne says – to "unreflectively believe everything that is attributed to music's miraculous effects." It's not only the proximity of many music therapists to singing bowls, vibrant energy and chakras that blurs the verifiable and unverifiable. Some of the core statements of psychoanalysis and psychotherapy have been repeatedly criticized as empirically untenable.[13]

By cultural comparison, in the study of early childhood development and the evaluations of music in psychology, neuroscience and ethology, some of the classified terms that fall under "specific behavior types" are also quite frequently and clearly characterized as anthropological constants: the caring, interested attention of the mother, the self-representation of the "soloists," the ritualized sung speech and the rhythmic synchronization of movements, voices or instruments. This distinction in the fundamental forms of musical communication and the differentiated perception of individual skills that make up human musicality (singing voice, relative pitch, feel of rhythm) could serve as a basis to better construct the sometimes nonspecific handling of "music" or "musical communication" as a therapeutic package recipe.

In this sense, particularly compelling are some modern forms of "functional" music therapy. These make targeted use of the neurobiological context of musical behavior and are mainly used in the field of neurological rehabilitation.

Sudden loss of brain function, which is usually caused by a disruption of the blood supply to the brain tissue, strikes a person like a lightning bolt out of the blue – hence the term "stroke." A common, very serious consequence of a stroke is *aphasia*, the loss of the ability to speak, read or write. Here, the typical speech regions in the left half of the brain are affected, including Broca's area, which controls language skills. However, patients with severe Broca's aphasia can still understand speech, but are barely able to speak coherently themselves.

There is no effective therapy for severe cases of aphasia. German neurologist Gottfried Schlaug has recently performed a study at Harvard Medical School, which has been used sporadically for several years now to return speech back to aphasics. It is based on the amazing observation that some people who have lost their ability to speak after a stroke are still able to sing songs with words. It is known that both halves of the brain are active in musical activity. The presumption now is that speech is controlled by the network in the right hemisphere of the brain when singing, which still functions even if Broca's area has failed. Everyone knows the experience of being able to sing a song from memory, but one falters as soon as one is supposed to deliver the text "in prose." People who stutter don't do so when they sing. Melody and rhythm drag the words along, so to speak.

In "melodic intonation therapy" (the name of the method studied at Harvard) patients initially learn to sing single words as specified by the therapist, which are then strung together into a simple sentence like "I am hungry." The singing is supported by rhythmic tapping with the left hand. Over the course of therapy, patients learn to separate sung words from melody and to speak "normally" again. They receive speech via a detour into singing. Using MRI scans, Schlaug proved that the brain's right hemisphere had actually assumed the functions of the damaged speech areas in the left hemisphere after seventy-five therapy sessions. Once the aphasia patient has put together a small collection of words, then the vocabulary can be expanded by continuing to use conventional speech therapy. Melodic intonation therapy is indeed tedious and requires a lot of patience, but relatives and friends of the patient can also learn the method and practice with them.

Other very common consequences of a stroke are movement disorders, which, for example, can affect walking or the use of hands. Neurological rehabilitation of patients with walking difficulties exploits the known phenomenon that rhythmic music acts as a strong stimulus for movement. Even simple periodic acoustic signals like the clicking of a metronome or special workout music with percussion instruments can stimulate the nerve system and act as time base for the steps of the patient, similar to dancing or marching. Even if the transmission paths between the auditory and motor pathways of the nervous system have not been clarified in detail, the effectiveness of *rhythmic acoustic stimulation* (RAS) in the rehabilitation of stroke patients has been proven in several studies. This form of therapy can also be applied in the treatment of Parkinson's disease, traumatic brain injury and infantile cerebral palsy.

"Musikunterstutztes Training" (music-assisted training) was developed at Hannover's University of Music, Theatre and Media, and is another type of neurological music-therapy used to treat hand paralysis which uses musical instruments as training tools. The patient tries to play a melody on the piano or beat a rhythm on a drum with the stroke-affected hand in order to reclaim control over the paralyzed limb. The secret to this method is explained by the fact that the patient receives immediate feedback of his movements through the sound. What happens here is also explained by musician's studies: when practicing the piano or violin, your hearing must control the complex movements of your hands in "real time." When playing an instrument, new nerve connections, which improve dexterity, are created in the brain. The therapy concurrently motivates patients to actively cope with their motor skill disorder. Studies show that music-assisted therapy benefits patients faster than conventional physiotherapy. Their movements become faster and they are able to perform daily activities again.

Does Mozart Make You Smart?

After an overview of the effects of music on the organism and visits to the practice rooms of various music therapy applications, it is time to take stock.

It has been shown that the potential of the therapeutic use of music, its strengths and weaknesses, are better understood if we see music therapy against the backdrop of the "nature of music" that exists in us biologically – and against the background of what we know today. We have seen that listening to music can have strong mental and physical effects, from goosebumps to calming patients in ICU. Next, we can state that active handling of music (be it singing, playing or moving) in the therapeutic field brings along possiblities other than just listening. This is not surprising: those who watch a football game on TV will experience breathtaking emotional ups and downs under certain circumstances. However, in this way, they can't play football nor feel the tension of offense, defense and sportsmanship. For this they must play football themselves.

We can also speak more scientifically: the various psychophysical interactions involved in making music and listening support the basis of the assumption that any "class of behaviors" that we call music has emerged in human evolution as an integral part of our social and communicative behavior. This assumption in turn places the effects of music in a different light: the emotional "reward" that participation in music provides, the effect of singing on babies, the motor impulses triggered by rhythm or even reconnection with lost speech through singing, indicates that the ability of "musical speaking" represents itself in the brain.

Thus, the evolutionary theory of "what music is" is in many ways linked to findings on "how music works." Now, the only thing missing is the connection to cultural history, the changing superstructure weird construction. On the accelerated journey through the history of musical culture in Central Europe, especially in Germany, in the second chapter of this book I have tried to present how people of our cultural area have tended to handle music socially through the centuries. The European musical culture had to and has to endure tensions and contradictions, despite – or because of – its glamourous sophistication: literate, spiritual erudition distanced itself from the musical tradition of the masses. Forms broke away from their original functional context and became "musical art," which was performed by professional musicians for a consuming audience. Finally, music emancipated itself from? time, space and people, and became a transportable object.

It's probably not unreasonable to note that social heydays are associated with a (re)convergence of musical contrasts. Ancient Athens is both the archetype of a community of enlightened ideas as well as the source of all Western philosophical and scientific approaches. Could it be a coincidence that music theory, pedagogy, active music-making and archaic and refined forms of music were closely linked to ancient Greece through their nonmusical functions and concept of society?

In the European Middle Ages, spiritual high art separated from people's musicality, and during the time of absolutism, professionals from the secular music world also parted from the audience. In retrospect, we evaluate both eras as times of social depression. With the Enlightenment and the rise of the bourgeoisie as a supporting layer of a democratic society, musical life's opposites, the "above" and "below," as well as the musically active and passive roles, influenced and penetrated each other, which – at least partly – contributed to new national cultural identities.

Since the biological dimensions of music, as part of our nature, have a phenomenal effect in life and a role in culture and society, that is reason enough to treat music as an essential content in any event that we call "education." If one understands education as a holistic concept, then it seems obvious that musical skills must be encouraged in children and developed in upbringing, as well as other skills that are ingrained in us by nature: language, motor skills, logical thinking, social behavior and sense of responsibility must all be promoted and developed.

Music educators have largely been in agreement on this for decades. Fritz Jöde, one of the protagonists of the youth music movement of the early twentieth century, said, "Music is born and doesn't want to be known, recognized or mastered as such, but it wants to live and be lived." He called to his fellow countrymen, "Help me so that we become again singing people." In the 1920s, Leo Kestenberg, social democrat and music critic at the Prussian

Ministry of Science, Art and Education, transferred these reform ideas into concrete decrees. Because he placed "musical, vigorous human life above virtuosity and one-sidedness," and wanted to develop "talents in the open area of musical culture," he professionalized the training of music teachers, regulated the musical training of kindergarten teachers and anchored the subject of music (previously, there was only the subject of "singing" in school) in teaching programs of all types of schools. Thanks to the Kestenberg reform, there are now state-trained and certified music teachers as there are teachers of other subjects.

Well-known composer and music educator Cesar Bresgen, who also emerged from the Youth Music Movement, wrote in his 1975 publication a "critical protocol" for music education: "We believe to have sufficiently substantiated which role music plays in human life. Thus, it is without a doubt that there *must* also be education that enables people to participate in music, wherein 'music' is understood not as some sound, but as a cultural component."[14]

Recently, Hans Günther Bastian, a professor of music education at the University of Frankfurt, said,

> Making music and a musician's life is a special way to exist in this "world" and to find oneself through it; that is, music is a medium and part of human self-realization, a basic state of the tuned and sounding human-in-the-world. [...] Music is our chance for human personalization, "a defined I." Music is therefore more than luxury and decor. And music is certainly more than the cultural "icing on the cake" in everyday life; it's the indispensable elixir of life. [...] And no question: there is "musicality" in each child if whether they know it and want it or not. We only need to allow it![15]

It seems almost everything is in order. Professionals and those responsible agree that music belongs to the people and emphasize its place in upbringing and education, both in terms of an education *in* music as well as an education *through* music.

But exhortation and urgency must be read in between the lines of Bresgen and Bastian. Apparently, there was and still is a shortcoming that should be remedied. A certain urgency to argue for the importance of music in the education canon is probably also, just like today's intensified search for the "beneficial" effects of music education on the child and its development, in the spirit of Plato. A much-debated question is: does music make one more intelligent? You may have missed this popular subject among the discussed effects of music, but it is specifically related to the question of the meaning of music education.

In 1993, a message went through the press that caused a worldwide sensation. American psychologist Frances Rauscher had played a piano sonata by Mozart to her students and then asked them to perform tasks using spatial-visual imagination. The tests served to find out what patterns emerge when a sheet of paper is folded, twisted and cut in a certain way. Rauscher's findings from the students who had listened to Mozart for ten minutes were 8 to 9 IQ points higher than the results of the group of students who merely relaxed and also in comparison to other subjects that listened to so-called *minimalist* music by Philip Glass.

The significant public interest in the study is not surprising because both pedagogy as well as the music industry sought to gain great profits from the so-called Mozart effect, as the phenomenon was thereafter called. After all, the study was published in the prestigious journal *Nature* – the *Vogue* of scientists. It even made waves in politics: on 13th January 1998, the Governor of Georgia commenced a program giving away free classical CDs to every new mother in the state in order to increase the intelligence of their child.

Rauscher's study led to numerous follow-up studies in which her experiments were replicated in one way or another, but the alleged Mozart effect only occasionally affirmed itself. One also gladly overlooked that Rauscher had only detected a short-term effect of music on a small aspect of intelligence, namely proven spatial-visual tasks. In 1999, the euphoria received a severe setback when the data from sixteen studies on the relationship between listening to music and intelligence was reanalyzed. This revealed that overall, on average only a very small effect was detected, which was well below a person's IQ fluctuations, determined on the "daily condition," of about 4.5 points. In 2010, Viennese psychologist Jacob Pietschnig and his staff subjected the Mozart effect to their own evaluation in another meta-analysis, using data of more than 3,000 subjects from thirty-nine studies that had been conducted so far. This did not show a statistically significant increase of intelligence through listening to Mozart's (or other) music.

These results don't diminish the beauty and sensuality of Mozart's compositions in any way, and should not interfere with our motivation to listen to his music with pleasure and perhaps play it ourselves.

However, these results probably mean waving goodbye to the wishful thinking that one can create better-functioning people simply by administering beautiful music like a drug without too vague having to do something about it themselves.

Even more justified, from an anthropological and educational point of view, is the idea of examining the significance of active music learning and the making of music in the development of children.

The most prominent study performed in this context was led by Hans Guenther Bastian and his staff between 1992 and 1998 at Berlin's primary schools. A total of 170 children from seven different primary schools were recruited for this study. 130 children received two hours of music lessons in their schools per week learned an instrument individually or in groups and made music in ensembles. A control group of forty children received only one hour of "normal" music education per week as part of the general primary education. Scientists studied intelligence, social behavior and concentration of all students for a period of several years. After three years of observation there was barely any difference between the IQ development of the two groups. However, after four years, the students in music classes showed a slight increase in intelligence of an average 6 IQ points.

Regardless, the result is affected by several methodological criticisms regarding the conduct of the study. Some of Bastian's colleagues complained, in particular, that the control group (i.e., the group of children with "normal" primary education) was much smaller than the music group. A further point of criticism, was that the children in the control group received no additional lessons in a different area, Bastian disagreed with this claim, since the two classes were either speech- or sports-oriented.

Bastian's study received a positive response from the general public, whose feedback was of course influenced by popular simplifications in the media. In sum: a tendency is evident, but the all-too-high expectations and wishful thinking that music lessons will make children smarter and improve their overall school performance could not be met by the Bastian study, nor by other similar studies.

Another effect of increased music education was nevertheless clearly recognizable: children in music classes showed improved social behavior and more developed social skills – they rarely excluded other students. If one wants to address the "nonmusical" benefits in order to argue for an increase in music lessons at school, then this effect especially should come to light existentially, considering the massive integration deficits, propensity for violence and social neglect that have been significantly exacerbated in German schools since 1998, when the Bastian study ended.

Against the background of human ethological observation and the probable evolutionary role of musical behavior, the idea that music could or should improve cognitive performance in other areas is not necessarily plausible. Musical behavior has mainly to do with social and family ties, the ability of communication and expression – and a little bit with what we may call self-expression or self-realization. A relationship between musicality and nonmusical intellectual or technical performance is not explicitly recognizable in an overall anthropological picture. A fugue by Bach is certainly a complex structure that requires a high degree of mathematical intellect, but a peak artistic performance is not the goal of music education in school. Presumably, the idea that one can also achieve better math grades by reading music ultimately leads back to the speculative *Musica universalis* thinking of ancient times. However, the observation that music education can improve social behavior fits perfectly with the behavioral biological knowledge of music as being "social glue."

But what are the reasons the intense search justifications music education, *more* music education in our modern society in which music seems so ubiquitous? The hope for nonmusical benefits in times of PISA studies and ADHD is one motive. However, the other reason lies in the changes of how we deal with music: changes that – although they are not recognizable for each of us individually – can be described as a landslide without exaggeration.

A teacher from a small town in Upper Bavaria reports on the traditional parade on St Martin's Day, 11th November, where children roam through town in the evenings with their lanterns and sing songs according to the ancient custom. "In the past, all children sang in the St Martin's parade," says the teacher, "and they knew all the songs by heart: 'Saint Martin, Saint Martin, I Walk with My Lantern' and more. A few years ago someone brought a portable CD player to the lantern parade. A CD with St Martin songs played and the children sang along. Nowadays only the CD plays and the children themselves don't sing anymore."

This anecdote is not unique. Musicologists and educators verify the "loss of singing in the everyday culture" of our society.[16] According to studies by music sociologist Karl Adamek, the percentage of primary school pupils that can sing a simple melody has dropped since 1970 from about 90 per cent to about 10 per cent. Such figures are difficult to verify, but well-known children's voice trainer and songbook author Andreas Mohr, after decades of professional experience, comes to this conclusion: "Many children in Germany cannot sing – and the worst part is that today's music teachers cannot either." Mohr sees the problem not only in the fact that children know fewer and fewer songs from home, kindergarten or school, but also in the fact that they use their vocals in an unhealthy way. If teachers sing at all with kindergarten children, then they do it – because they themselves have too little singing experience – in their speaking voice, which is too low for children to properly and healthily sing along with.[17]

According to music teacher Beate Quaas, many teachers have a broken relationship with music: "They almost emphasize their singing disability as self-protection. At the same time, however, an immense desire to sing exists." An insert in the *Frankfurter Rundschau* reads, "The conditions in a Hamburg kindergarten are symptomatic: here, teachers master only one song, namely the popular song 'Die Affen rasen durch den Wald' ('The Monkeys Race through the Forest'). This song is sung in a low, unhealthy way for children and is struck up at every opportunity."

Specialists in voice and speech disorders estimate that the frequency of certain voice disorders in children (induced by improper use of the voice), lies in the frightening ballpark of 20 to 30 per cent. Regardless, waiting rooms of phoniatrists and speech therapists are still not crowded with hoarse children. This would require that someone notices the disorder and recognizes it as such.

Leipzig choirmaster Georg Christoph Biller (Johan Sebastian Bach's current successor at St Thomas Church) characterizes social singing development with one sentence: "One no longer sings oneself, one lets others do that." In elementary school, children will only be adequately challenged musically when they accidentally get one of the few teachers with a music education as classroom teacher. This condition causes Professor Hans Günther Bastian, as well as the Speaker at the Baden-Württemberg Rectors Conference and the Managing Director of the German Orchestra Association in Berlin, to come independently to the opinion that more and more children, according to their findings, leave school "musically illiterate."

How could this have happened? How could this ancient human behavior and need – which was, especially in Germany, over the last two hundred years so passionately loved and dearly kept – become so lost?

Adorno and the Consequences

Our journey through cultural musical history ended rather abruptly somewhere in the twentieth century in the second part of this book. There, we had to step aside to orient ourselves in the area – and now? we must check out the ground more precisely and follow the forks in the road to understand what was just mentioned.

In artistic salons, at home on pianos and in the singing clubs of the German empire, civic life around 1900 was actively musical. The amateur could adopt art music, and art music adopted folk music. From this democratization of music and from the first wave of "folklore" also sprouted a new musical movement where young people would wander from the gray city walls out into nature, singing and playing a guitar, thus setting themselves apart from the national frolicking in the singing clubs of the Wilhelmine period.

The youth music movement first went hand in hand with the *Wandervogel* (a German youth club) and later became independent. In 1909, medical student Hans Breuer published the songbook *Zupfgeigenhansl*, a collection of 300 folk songs with chord symbols for accompaniment on the guitar (*Zupfgeige*). It is no coincidence that the singing movement formed around the same time as the Boy Scouts, education reform, the natural food movement, nudism, art nouveau and the expressionist Der Blaue Reiter (The Blue Rider) group. Its lifestyle was anything but old-fashioned and bourgeois, preserving the old master's standing and upholding folk songs as authentic expressions of the "indestructible life force." By the early 1930s *Zupfgeigenhansl* had already reached a circulation in the millions.

The most famous protagonist of the singing movement was Fritz Jöde from Hamburg. He founded the first music school and shortly after the First World War started the so-called Musicians Guild, which organized countrywide singing and playing circles with musical practice and theory as well as open singing lessons. That's how the self-image of the youth music movement expanded from the Wandervogel to a claim on public education. Along with Kestenberg's reform of music teaching, what? greatly influenced the training of public school teachers which, in turn, was largely designed by Jöde as a professor at the State Academy for Church and School Music in Berlin.

The singing movement continued far into West Germany's postwar period. The conviction that folk songs and self-directed and playful learning should be a core content of school music education, in the sense of a child-friendly, holistic arts education, remained for a long time. The textbook *Der Musikant* (The musician), edited by Fritz Jöde, was still in use in classrooms during the 1960s. During this time schools were also equipped with Orff's *Schulwerk*, a modular system of xylophones and percussion for elementary music lessons.

I went to elementary school in Munich in the 1970s: twice a year, all the students would gather in the gym where, amidst the many blue mats on which we children sat, there was a pedestal where Rector Feldmann used to sit with his guitar. Feldmann, a robust, gray-haired man in his mid-fifties, spent the morning singing common folk songs with the whole school, repeating them so many times until all the children knew the songs. A highlight of the event was "Jetzt fahr'n wir übern See" ("Now we ride over the lake"), because the last word of each verse could only be sung in the next repetition; the first time one tried one had to close one's mouth very quickly. It never quite worked all the time, which drove Feldix (as we called him) up the wall.

Despite his somewhat rude manner, all the songs remained with us. Once, Feldix practiced three songs in succession, then divided the entire group of children into three smaller groups and instructed us to sing "O du lieber Augustin," "Heißa Kathreinerle" and "Lass doch der Jugend ihren Lauf" at the same time. I was completely fascinated by how the miracle worked and began to suspect that the three songs were probably constructed in a similar pattern.

We were still singing "Tanz mit der Dorle, walz mit der Dorle, bis nach Schweinau mit der Dorle" ("Dance with Dorle, roll with Dorle, off to Schweinau with Dorle") on our way home. We laughed so hard about "Schweinau" (which literally means "pig meadow") and did not realize that Feldix was probably far and wide the last guitar principal, and that Dorle had long since retired.

A damning verdict from Frankfurt ushered of whom? farewell, which rang in the ears of teachers and civil servants in the ministries of education: "Nowhere is it written that singing is necessary." claimed the sociologist Theodor Wiesengrund Adorno in 1956 in his treatise "*Kritik des Musikanten*" (Criticism of musicians; referring also to Jöde's *Der Musikant*). In 1956, Adorno's opinion didn't find too much resonance in music education, but it did so ten years later because the Marxist leader of the Frankfurt Institute for Social Research was considered one of *the* leaders of the so-called '68 generation and significantly influenced sociotheoretical reorientation and reinterpretation in the Federal Republic. Even his music theoretical and music aesthetical opinions have influenced, and still influence, the far-reaching intellectual understanding of music. Adorno went against the singing movement and minstrelsy vehemently. The concept of a musician is the "secret precedence of making music over music; that the one that fiddles should be more important than what he fiddles." The concept of practice is "in its abstractness no better than that of the self-sufficient theory." The "affirmation of the activity as such" is dubious; according to Adorno, the desired joy in music is infantile: "Their habits remind of a puberty that is frozen and declared as programmatic." The social scientist accused the music movement of "taking art away from art," and being "boastfully close to nature [...], making a great honor out of the contempt of allegedly bourgeois forms because the happiness of the form itself, without which there is no art, becomes stunted."[18]

What prompted Adorno to this contemptuous judgment and what prompted the scientific community to listen to Adorno? The answer is, as so often in Germany: the Third Reich. The Nazis had indeed first removed Fritz Jöde from his office, but at the same time incorporated the forms and contents of the youth music movement (and youth movement in general) and made them ideologically beneficial. Community singing was upheld at school and in the Hitler Youth, and the Nazi-controlled leisure organization Kraft durch Freude (Strength through Joy) staged "open singing" and "song hours of the people." After the German catastrophe, especially after the disillusion of national ideology, shouldn't everything exemplary of folk be inevitably suspicious? Undeniably, according to Adorno. Folk music shared a "commonality with fascism in key positions: the appeal to the so-called youth, both as a dynamic and socially vague group; the ingratiation with the people and their supposedly ideal or naturalistic strength; the precedence of the collective over the individual; the defamation of the intellect no less than of the senses and of any subjective differentiations the tried and tested method to trumpet the regressions as original and more real, as even more advanced than the progress."

Around 1970, music education professors like Michael Alt, Dankmar Venus or Heinz Antholz worked up Adorno's guiding principles for school. Alt criticized music education for its "tireless urge for technical skills, even if they are achieved in artistically inferior objects." For that one renounces "to a large extent discussions of work and general educational efforts to awaken an understanding in the child and adolescent." Alt called for a reorientation of school music education in which social singing must "be kept within limits," compared to listening to artistically challenging pieces, which elevates itself as a "free mental activity" over the "foot stand of music."[19] Even in the latter requirement he followed Adorno, for whom music education was meant to be an exclusively intellectual pursuit, even in terms of the emancipation of the individual in "the silent reading of music." The social philosopher even believed that the instructions for score reading or the explanations of the clef and transposition could exert a "colorful attraction" to children.

So, it seems the foundations on which new music education erected itself were basically the consequences of history and of an aesthetic sense of responsibility. But perhaps Adorno's aversion to everything that he called "music educational music," and especially his aversion to social singing, was not just politically motivated. A short, autobiographical confession in *"Kritik des Musikanten"* should be read carefully:

> The inhibition [to sing], which the youth movement removed, really had no bad reason, as we can hardly ignore this tone of violence, of bought courage, of impudence, in fresh spontaneous singing. I distinctly remember how embarrassing it was for me when my mother and her sister – both singers by profession – probably at the request of my father, started to sing "O Täler weit, o Höhen" ("O valleys far, o heights"). Singing as a piece of natural behaviour related to real situations instead of as objectified artwork [...] is shame."

These few words must speak volumes for psychologists. Perhaps young Theodore's primary school teacher should have encouraged him to simply sing along, thus taking away the child's feeling of embarrassment, and the postwar history of German music education might have progressed very differently.

However, the majority of the German teachers and educators went along with Adorno, rather than replying with confidence that singing is a spontaneous natural expression of life. In response to the question "Does singing make one stupid?" Helmut Segler designated singing in 1976 as "a practice that degrades the singer to an object, either to an object of timeless educational value and formal educational process or to the object of one's own unreflective emotion."[20]

Consequently, the purpose of teaching music at school was shifted from making music to listening to music; it was even proposed to rename the subject "auditory perception education." That is why we find scores by György Ligeti rather than German folk songs in West German music textbooks in primary schools during the 1970s. The reservations about singing songs encroached upon the private sphere and were nourished from the outside. In a 1973 music-themed guide for parents, Margrit Kuntzel-Hansen wrote,

> Music is for most parents synonymous to singing. And for a long time, practicing folk and children's songs was the only possible starting point for musical education. Nowadays, this view is obsolete. Singing songs plays only a minor role. [...] The world of old folk and children's songs has less and less in common with the today's world. The treasury of songs in songbooks remained unaffected by the changing times. Yet, it still says, "in March the farmer saddled the steed," even though every child knows that most farmers use a tractor on their land.[21]

Küntzel-Hansen went on to say that children are tired of singing and repeating songs that have no reference to their imagination and would rather invent new songs with a current vocabulary, such as "highway, bicycle, computer, escalator, flea market, typewriter, astronaut, etc." Therefore, she wrote *Liedercommode* (*The Song Chest*), a modern songbook in which characters, word fragments, sounds and exclamations are printed as if it were a comic, and with which the children are allowed to improvise freely.

"BOOOOONG, BOOOONG, BOOOONG," sounds the thunder; the rain beats "PLOP PLOP PLOP," and finally the fire department approaches with "TA TÜ TA TA." There is no doubt that such improvisations can stimulate playfulness and imagination. However, they hardly do the musical potential and vocal abilities of children justice.

These efforts reveal the efforts to supply a need for common, convivial, expressive singing with light, innocuous fare. The nature of anthropological universals – any habit that people in all cultures and even small children display – means that they cannot be eradicated quickly. Therefore, more and more songs found admission into West German education in the 1980s and 1990s, especially foreign folklore and spiritual songs, because the distrust of the German folk song was ongoing. Even during the 1980s, Jochen Unbehaun ranted in a didactic book for music teachers about "the still-haunting idea of 'artistic education'" and explains that the "singing of songs" had served for centuries mainly to indoctrinate students. Interestingly, in the same book Unbehaun passionately advocates the study and performance of the American civil rights movement song "We Shall Overcome" as a "direct expression of a society that is ready for action."[22]

However, the GDR never broke the tradition of singing songs. Firstly, collective singing has proven itself to be an instrument of ideological consonance of whatever color, and secondly, one was indisputably aware of the social democratic roots that the youth music movement of the 1920s had. What an irony of history that this movement was defamed as "cultural Bolshevism" after 1933 and "prefascist" after 1945.

After all that, it is no coincidence that the generation of today's thirty- to fifty-year-olds has little joy for singing and, as choir associations state, is rarely represented in choirs. A large extent of this generation didn't grow up with an everyday culture of singing. The consequences reach even further, because these thirty- to fifty-year-olds are also parents, educators and teachers that share their musical behavior with today's children. Those who grow up with the opinion that singing is rather embarrassing and ridiculous will have a hard time singing a song to their children or to a class.

But we should not hold Adorno and his disciples solely responsible for the "musical illiteracy" and "singing crisis" that music educators lament. Adorno, who died in 1969, saw *the one* great conflict between naïve, "loden jacket style" singing and fiddling on the one side, and the intellectual examination of the work of art, especially with Schoenbergian avant-garde on the other side. Adorno feared that the singing movement tradition was what kept the youth from art and intellectual maturity. However, Adorno only took marginal notice of a third, much broader tendency, which was neither folksy not artsy: pop culture and its music. Maybe he did not want to recognize it as the true modern counterpart to high culture *and* folk music because it was politically contentious: Adorno despised jazz and all popular music – which he called "amusement music" – but also the Nazis reviled jazz as "degenerate music," just as they did the new music that Adorno adhered to. Therefore, the aesthetic position of the Frankfurt sociologist can not generally be regarded as a liberal, democratic counterpoint to the cultural traditionalism and nationalism of the Third Reich. It is rather a very personal, exclusive view and yet it was made cultural policy.

Turning On and Turning Off

We only briefly illuminated three places in the terrain of the musical landscape of the twentieth century: the first was the presentation of a device to record and reproduce sounds in a newsroom in New York City (in the nineteenth century), then there was the separation of *new music* from the Western music tradition of the past 2,500 years. A third spotlight fell on the scene of the small but significant misunderstanding of what "modern music" is. Where is the topographic connection between these events?

After Arnold Schönberg and other musical revolutionists broke away from musical tradition, *new music* (the "serious music" of the twentieth century) only reached a very small part of the audience, an intellectual elite if you will, that was willing to carry out an aesthetic paradigm change and let go of harmonious perceptions. The "conservative" majority of the concert audience (and therefore also the concert promoters that depended on the market) stuck to the music of past decades and centuries, which was soon declared to be a timeless corpus of "classical" music. Modern "classicists" such as Hindemith, Strawinsky or Bartók, who tied their composing style to the classical tradition and processed elements of folk music, were also still popular. But in the aerial image of the modern musical landscape it is hard to see how the new, very different river, which was initially fed by tributaries of jazz and music hall entertainment, formed its bed, gained momentum and width and became the world's mainstream in the 1960s: popular music.

Definitions are always problematic, any musical demarcation is contestable, but here I denote popular or pop music (a better collective term has not yet been invented) to be a youth-specific, Anglo-American style of music born after 1945, which uses continuous drum foundations, tonal harmony, electrically amplified instruments and equally amplified singing voices. This music became, quantitatively speaking, the representative of "modern" music in the late twentieth and early twenty-first centuries, taking the place of the broad-based, modern continuation of European art music. This is a singular event in the history of music. After centuries of ever-changing and ever-new inflows, the flow of occidental art music dries up almost completely and is replaced by two entirely contradictory flows, both of which have no tradition: new atonal music and popular music.

The triumph of pop takes place simultaneously with that of television and the enormous expansion of the sound recording industry. This is no coincidence, as media shape the development and the aesthetics of popular music. Rock without an electric guitar and without a microphone would be like a classical symphony without strings. The music industry thrives mainly on the marketing of popular music: pop and mass media have a symbiotic relationship. Of the 147 million CDs that were sold in Germany in 2009, the proportion of "pop" (i.e., rock, pop and dance), was about 69 percent. Classical accounted for 7.8 percent; the rest were audio books, jazz, folk music and children's CDs.

In addition to the digital successor of the record, other forms of music media have captured the distribution market in recent decades. 1981 saw the debut of MTV and the popularization of the video clip. MTV is now aired in most countries of the world. Since the beginning of the private use of the Internet in the 1990s, the PC (available today in at least 80 percent of households in the developed world) has played an increasingly important role in the purchasing, listening and reproduction of music.

To answer our question of what else, apart from Adorno's singing taboo, could have contributed to taking away people's voices, one should look here. The anecdote of the children at the St Martin's Day parade, who play a CD rather than sing, is illustrative of the problem: music is nowadays primarily a "listening product." Until the invention of the phonograph, all music was live music. However, sound carriers, "canned music," made listening entirely independent from the location and time of the event. Technology made it possible to listen to music wherever and whenever we want. Thus, due to advancing technical developments, it has become increasingly common to purchase music as an industrially manufactured product and increasingly unusual to actively participate in its production or be there "live." We should also remember that not too long ago one swung one's legs in a local dance hall mostly to music played by a band. The wave of discotheques, where one dances to LP music, only took off during the 1970s.

The typical modern way to handle music is to listen to sound recordings. This is not only true for a Mozart piano concerto at teatime or the newest title of the latest popular band, but also for art and entertainment music, as technically perfect as possible (understandably). But the tendency of the finished product also affects colloquial singing and making music, as the St Martin's Day parade example shows. Some modern mothers play a soothing CD to their baby instead of singing a lullaby. Of course this trend runs parallel to other areas of life in industrial society: those who only buy jam in the supermarket, and have only ever known of jam as a purchased product, will not be easily motivated to pick cherries from a tree or from the ground, wash them, pit them, examine them for worms, boil the fruit with sugar and various ingredients into a preserve and eventually fill sterilized canning jars.

The easier it is to handle the media and the smaller the playback devices, the lower the dependency on certain places, situations and times when listening to music. In 1979, Sony introduced the first Walkman to the market, a pocket-sized cassette player with headphones. The Walkman made it possible to listen to music almost anywhere, even in public, in the presence of other people, without disturbing them. By 2004, Sony had distributed about 335 million cassette players worldwide. Digital MP3 players, which weigh less than cassette devices and have far more technical possibilities, have had an even faster circulation. The American manufacturer of the iPod, Apple, sold 100 million units worldwide within just five years. Nowadays, about 80 percent of German teenagers own an MP3 player and most of them use it daily or at least several times a week.

These devices make it possible to always have music with you wherever you go. They are so small that they don't even restrict the freedom of movement in sports and have so much memory that only the battery charge limits the playing time. Nowadays, one will meet several young people on any city bus or subway car listening to music in this way, oblivious to their environment. One secondary school teacher reported that the students of his ninth-grade class come with "buttons in their ears" to school in the morning. They reluctantly turn off the device at the beginning of class and immediately turn it back on during breaks and after school.

This self-chosen musical companionship mixes into the acoustic environment of daily life, over which the individual usually has little influence. However, this environment is increasingly filled with music also. Let us accompany Frank Schneider, our passionate Mozart listener, a little.

After tea, Frank remembers that he must go to the hairdresser, so that he may look presentable when he meets his new female colleague for dinner. He doesn't need an appointment at the hairdresser around the corner. Frank enters the salon; ahead of him only one customer is waiting, so it won't take long. He takes a seat on the waiting bench, although the music that is playing in the salon bothers him. He finds the rhythm aggressive and scrolls through a women's magazine. After a few minutes it is his turn. While the young female hairdresser cuts his hair she suddenly says to her colleague at the neighboring chair: "Oh, this song is so cool!" Frank Schneider briefly listens and thinks: *Yeah, not too bad – but I wouldn't want to listen to that all day!* On the way back home Frank makes a quick stop at the supermarket to buy a few things for next day's breakfast. He puts a loaf of bread, coffee and a jar of jam into the cart; he also grabs some muesli and asks for some slices of ham at the meat counter. Then he simply proceeds to the checkout and pays. Frank hasn't even noticed the quiet Whitney Houston song that was playing in the supermarket. At home he takes a shower, checks out his haircut in the mirror, puts on something suitable and goes to his dinner date. He heads to the nearest subway station. On the platform he hears or detects classical music running in the background: Vivaldi, *The Four Seasons*. It registers with Frank and he feels quite comfortable with it. Allegedly, classical music is supposed to expel homeless people and junkies from the station he has read, but he doesn't think that it works; they're still around. He enters the subway car, sits down and looks out the window.

Even before the train starts to move he notices a monotonous, rhythmic hissing. It comes from the earphones of the young man sitting across from him, who is wired to a cell phone. Frank is upset about the lack of consideration, but he doesn't say anything, and moves to another seat. A few weeks ago he read in the newspaper that teenagers attacked a man because he had asked them to turn their music down. Even from a seat further away he can still hear the *sh-t-ss – sh-t-ss* and he is glad that he only has to ride to the next station.

At Alfredo's, the Italian restaurant, Frank doesn't have to wait long for Lydia, his charming colleague. Lydia finds that Eros Ramazzotti, who can be heard playing in the background, goes very well with the saltimbocca and Montepulciano. However, Frank thinks that he would rather replace it with Vivaldi or mandolin music as accompaniment. Later, they arrange to meet at Lydia's next time and cook together. Frank promises to bring along some music.

Why does music play in department stores, fashion boutiques, salons, cafés, restaurants, hotel lobbies and gyms? What function does it fulfill there and how is it perceived? Let's ask around a bit.

The hotel receptionist explains that the gentle, meditative background music, which sprinkles over her working area, is to create a relaxed atmosphere for guests. The music is free from royalty license fees and is specifically produced for hotel and restaurant sound systems. The receptionist perceives these New Age sounds as rather "soporific." However, she doesn't want to work completely without music either, something should be playing in the background. She would rather have a stimulating rhythm.

A law student has recently started working in a small espresso bar in the hall of a university building, turns on a CD player. Why, because she herself likes to listen to music at work? No, her boss demands it; their guests should feel comfortable. It has been agreed with the university's management. Now, whoever is standing behind the counter can decide what to play. However, it shouldn't be too aggressive, so no techno, the student explains.

According to popular belief, background music in department stores enhances the shopping desire of customers. So, would Frank Schneider have put muesli in his cart without Whitney Houston? According to a study performed in 1982 by American marketing professor Ronald E. Milliman, customers stay longer in stores with quiet music. However, other research studies could not confirm this effect. The question of whether the investment in a music system, speakers and reproduction rights is worthwhile for retailers therefore remains unclear.

It is clear that the new stream has been widely adopted into the landscape. An older employee at a supermarket in Munich complains about the constant pop music that "toots" at her workplace. However, the managing director of the chain says that they play music because all supermarkets do it, just not discount stores, which they want to set themselves apart from. He doesn't believe it increases sales, but it creates a friendly atmosphere. Previously, music in shopping areas was louder, but employees and customers complained and so the volume was reduced. The music should be discreet, unobtrusive, yet stimulating. Lounge music is therefore out of the question, also no classical, which would be too one-sided and won't address the majority of customers. One rather listens to classical music at home with a glass of wine, the supermarket manager thinks.

On the other hand, transportation departments of some large cities have been filling underground stations with classical music for several years now, in part to keep homeless people, drug addicts and violent adolescents away. There are no reliable reports on this system's success. The Munich transportation department, MVG, admits that Vivaldi and Beethoven are supposed to transfer a "subjective sense of security." In fact, according to a survey, 20 percent of male and 30 percent of female passengers feel more protected against violent attacks on a platform where "civilized" music is played.

Background music in public is appreciated by some people, barely consciously perceived by many, missed by some if it is not played, perceived by some as disturbing and sharply criticized by others as acoustic pollution. "Acoustic space is common ground. It belongs to everyone!" according to the preamble of a petition to the German parliament, in which an association named Pipedown asked the government to ensure that the legal provisions for the protection of citizens against unwanted and avoidable sound will be greatly improved in regards to recorded music.

Let's realize a neutral fundamental thought at the end of this section: music, originally a means of communication from person to person, breaks away from its origin through the medium of a sound carrier: the receiver (the listener) can consume the music spatially and temporally independent from the transmitter (the performer), where and when he wants, just by turning on a device. But, when music recordings are used in public to produce an acoustic environment, then the music also separates from the receiver. The random listener usually *uses* this acoustic environment unintentionally (i.e., they are not visiting to listen or dance to music, they are merely exposed to it). In this form, music plays a similar role in our lives as good or bad weather, smog, floral scents or the smell of feces.

Persona

"Music and Person" is the heading of the large chapter that comes to an end here. It revolves around the question: what does music do with a person, with an individual? What does the individual do with music?

Our society is often accused – probably not without reason – of being either driven by pleasure or by utilitarianism. That music can serve the first is beyond question. However, the latter may be the reason for the renewed increase of interest in the "nonmusical" effects of music on the body, psyche and spirit.

Because health, educational and social benefits of singing and music-making are not obvious (though the economic benefits of the consumption of music as a product are clear), we look for scientific evidence for any nonartistic value of music, which we have always believed would be recognized by our instincts and intuition. But our enlightened rationalistic society no longer trusts in intuition, it demands to see proof and thus places itself into a forced justification for something that should be a natural part of life.

Nevertheless, it is wrong to glorify music as a universal remedy. Those effects that are either scientifically detectable, or at least in many cases observable, are often explained by specific functional contexts of musical behavior, which have grown during the evolution of man. The knowledge of these relationships teaches us that it is far from irrelevant what kind of music a person listens to or makes, or when and where this occurs. Also, in regard to today's particularly hot issue of education, do these anthropological contexts help in the orientation of the question: what can we expect from music as a means and object of education?

Here are some answers: we can't hope for some instillation of intelligence from listening to music and "auditory perception education," only a guide for conscious, distinctive listening and enjoyment. Active singing and music should not be used as a means to increase performance in other subjects or as prestigious accessory. Rather, it is a much more essential part of communication, of social interaction, of expression and of the development of the natural talent of a person. These are the effects that we can expect in good spirit and conscience from music education, from *musical* education.

Where the term "person" actually originates from is worth a note in this context. *Persona* is the Latin word for theater mask, through which aperture the voice of the actor sounds (*personat*). Therefore, our concept of person and personality initially depends etymologically on the tone of the voice. This is no accident; the voice is the medium through which we mainly express ourselves and impart ideas – linguistically, emotionally and musically. The "music-playing man" (as coined by the music anthropologist, Wolfgang Suppan in his book *Der musizierende Mensch*) is therefore first and foremost a singing man.

When Yehudi Menuhin used the motto "Singing is the true mother tongue of men" for his foundation to promote music education, the great violinist was thereby not a subject of any romantic transfiguration: the chant and the lullaby of the mother is the earliest musical experience of the child. Its first musical expressions are short songs, and who is surprised that the greatest enthusiasm of adult music fans is still reserved for singers. The musical development of a person begins and always leads back to singing.

IV. Risk More Music

Resonance

Conscious Listening

Music is communication. Music is a part of human nature. Music is social glue. Music is ritual. Music is stimulus for our emotional life. Music is cultural home. Music is play. Music is an active agent. Music is a commodity.

Which phrase fits us closest? How do we deal with music ourselves? Can society set its own goal to deal with music more *consciously* – just as we encourage one another to eat more consciously, to use resources more consciously and treat our bodies more consciously? Let's start with listening. The reality is that we have not developed into singing people in the postmodern, information-driven society, but the majority of us have developed into people that *listen*. Does *listening* also mean *listening in* and *listening to*? How consciously do we listen, how awake is our perception? We prefer certain musical styles, are less interested in others and might reject some music styles categorically. Such preferences may simply be a matter of personal taste or habit. However, it is not uncommon for our tastes to be related to where we see ourselves and how we understand ourselves. People feel they belong to a subculture or social group through specific characteristics, codes and customs, and they set themselves apart from other groups by these characteristics. Musical preferences can clearly mark and signal group membership. This need for group identification is a part of who we are as people and is nothing negative. We accept it, but are we also interested in listening over the fence of the familiar? It might be worth it, and it opens our ears to previously "unheard of" forms of expression, as well as some surprising cross-style similarities.

A die-hard classical listener might possibly be amazed when he accidentally finds out that the song "A Whiter Shade of Pale" by the group Procol Harum was composed on a bass line that is influenced by Johann Sebastian Bach, or when he listens for the first time to electric guitar virtuoso Mark Knopfler. Opera enthusiasts who are fascinated by the subtle nuances of expression in the human voice might discover unexpected things in Frank Sinatra's recordings from the 1950s or in the vocal artistry of jazz singer Nnenna Freelon. Rock fans, for whom classical music is too boring, should listen to Vivaldi's *Four Seasons* or Stravinsky's *The Rite of Spring*, which at its premiere caused ladies to fall powerless to the ground.

So-called popular music has become the "true" modern music over the last five decades. It is not only the vast majority of people in Western industrialized countries that listen mainly to popular music. Anglo-American pop style has had unprecedented success throughout the world and is currently produced as a global product, with different local flavors on all continents.

Conservative cultural criticism of the manifestations of popular culture is nothing new and is often an expression of subjective evaluation. The judgment, for example, that popular music is "shallow" cannot be objectified because there is no universal, value-neutral definition of artistic depth. Even seemingly scientific statements that certain popular music styles make the listener aggressive or stupid can hardly be empirically substantiated. This behavior is similar to the popularized claim that Coca Cola can dissolve a steak (and therefore probably also the stomach). Those who sacrifice a beef steak and a liter of Coke for this experiment will find out that not much happens, except that neither look very appetizing after some time. This myth of the tissue-eating beverage springs from concern for the health of our youth. But, just as there are quite rational, science-based findings about the properties of certain foods and beverages, it is also possible here to determine some factual statements about popular music. The aesthetics of pop and rock music are inextricably linked to electronic amplification; an "unplugged" acoustic version of a song is a rarity. Technology increases the loudness of music at rock concerts, techno events and discos, but also often in MP3 players, to a level that can, with prolonged exposure, irreversibly damage the hearing organ in the inner ear. The Swiss Accident Insurance Fund recently pointed out that the music industry has increased the sound pressure of their products in the genres of rock and pop by an average of ten decibels (which means a tenfold increase in sound energy!) in the last twenty years – because loud music allegedly sells better.

Another characteristic of popular music, which most people are hardly aware of, relates to the use of the voice. By nature, men's voices are on average one octave lower than women's voices (see graphic on page X) since the male larynx grows much stronger during puberty due to the action of testosterone. Considered evolutionarily, the significant sex dimorphism of the voice is a strong sexual signal. In fact, several psychological studies have shown that women judge low voices in men to be more attractive and more dominant than high ones. While classical vocal music takes advantage of the physiological sex differences of the voice, because every unamplified voice is most efficient in its natural "home range," male and female pop and rock singers tend to sing almost in the same vocal range – gender-neutral, so to speak. Female pop singers usually use their low chest register and male pop singers usually use a very high area of their vocal range, predominantly falsetto. Even varied female voices such as those of Shakira, Annett Louisan and Lena Meyer-Landrut are common in similar that they sing in about the same tonal range as Michael Jackson, Eros Ramazzotti or the group Supertramp.

Why such aesthetics have developed may have different reasons – maybe ideals of androgyny and youthfulness, or even the proximity of high male voices to the scream. In any case, one consequence of this development is that many people's idea of singing and their own voice are heavily influenced today by the examples of popular music. We consciously or unconsciously imitate what we habitually listen to. This leads to typical voice patterns, particularly in adolescents and young adults: many male voices take on a high pitch when they sing, which is produced by applying pressure and raising the larynx, and often results in a slightly nasal tone. They tend to fade out the relaxed sonorous depth that actually exists in their vocal range. However, women's voices remain within the limits of the chest voice, or they sing "breathily," with lots of air consumption. The smooth head register, the spacious "upper level" of the female voice, remains unused.

This limited use of the voice and (as an engineer would say) poor "efficiency range" can be exploited by a microphone and electronic amplification; however, during unamplified singing the voice will quickly run into scale and strength limits. The "pop voice" is ill-advised, especially for those who sing with children at school or in kindergarten because it does not allow for the tonal range that is recommended for singing with children, nor does it create the necessary acoustic assertiveness that is needed (while speaking as well as singing). In the long term, breathiness and pressure burden the voice and lead to vocal disorders. Speech therapists, singing teachers and vocal doctors will all "sing a song about it." These problems, rather unfairly, relate more to women's voices than men's.

The main reason why popular music literally "moves" the masses is not its so-often-claimed simplicity. Even rock or techno can be complex. A common feature of almost all popular music is the solid foundation of drums, the *beat*, which highlights the meter. Pop music is pulse-emphasized music. We know that one of the pillars of our musicality is that we can synchronize ourselves motorically (and emotionally) to a meter and that incisive rhythms represent a strong incentive to move. The recipe to "pop up" other styles of music in order to make them more marketable consists therefore mainly in underlying *percussion* – which can be recognized both in so-called folk music, as well as in the hits of pianist Richard Clayderman or in the "baroque-style" group Rondo Veneziano.

These comments are not meant as a value judgment, but as an encouragement to listen consciously in order to better understand the "biomusical" signals that reach our unconscious.

A "conscious" approach to music does not require a music degree, but certain knowledge of some pieces and a sense of style cannot hurt when one uses music for specific public purposes. Several years ago, Deutsche Bahn advertised in a television commercial the comfortable traveling on an intercity express: a lady that is leaning back comfortably in the seat of a first-class compartment views the landscape flying by through the train window to the sound of classical string music. The scene makes a dignified first impression. However, those who recognize the few bars of the underlying music might get a shock: this train ride is accompanied by the beginning of "Lacrimosa" from Mozart's *Requiem*, the Mass for the Dead. Those knowledgeable about music also know: these particular bars of the unfinished "Lacrimosa" are the very last notes Mozart brought to paper before his untimely demise. Is it an omen for a terrible end to the train ride? It is highly unlikely that the advertising agency had this meaning in mind. Rather, they probably wanted to use classical music as a generic – one could also say meaningless – code for a well-maintained lifestyle, not knowing that this music conveys a contrary message to the classical connoisseur.

The decoupling of form and content is known to be a hallmark of postmodernism and has reached even the highest social circles. At the Grand Tattoo, the highest German military ceremony, at which the German President, Chancellor and Minister of Defense are released from office, the music corps of the German Armed Forces play. In addition to the prescribed ceremonial ingredients – a march, a chorale verse, followed by a prayer and the national anthem – the to-be honorable person may choose three pieces of music that are appropriate for the event out of the so-called serenade. Chancellor Gerhard Schröder chose for his farewell in 2005 "The Ballad of Mack the Knife" by Kurt Weill, "Summertime" by George Gershwin and the famous hit "My Way" by Frank Sinatra. One might debate here whether the outgoing Chancellor displayed stylistic ignorance or deliberately chose the music to break through the highly military, religious and patriotic character of the ceremony. But then he could have dispensed with the ritual entirely and invite guests on a cruise, as did President Heinemann.

For Each Child Ten Songs

The present reality of a predominantly passive, more or less consciously consuming musical behavior stands in contrast to the realization that music is originally not a product nor entertainment nor a work of art, but communication. We can almost say with certainty that man has not developed another structured acoustic communication system in addition to language in the course of his evolutionary history "just for fun" – although fun is the best motivation to use it. The different behaviors that we call music have originated as specific "strategies" out of social interaction. In the process we call culture, they have separated from their original functions, in some cases rather far.

But what are we doing now with the discrepancy between today's musical reality and the knowledge of the "nature of music"? Does the "genetic clef" play a role at all in our life in the information society? Has our biologically inherited behavior not long since been transformed by cultural influences?

Modern man is always willing to reinvent the *conditio humana*, the human condition. He is caught up in a "self-spun web of significances," as anthropologist Clifford Geertz phrased it.[1] On the other hand, our genetic makeup is very close to that of the people who lived in the Hohle Fels in the Swabian Alps 30,000 years ago, who loved, had children and families, hunted, gathered, experienced happiness and distress, who rejoiced or were afraid, who had friends and enemies, and who fought and died. All that is directly related to our biology is nowadays not significantly different from our Stone Age ancestors: this is especially true for the physiology of body and brain, for the emotions that we show each other and the emotions with which we respond to our environment. In particular, our perception system and the triggering and control mechanism of our behavior is "archaically" calibrated.

For instance: when it comes to reaching a goal or receiving something, we do not like to wait, especially if others might beat us to the punch. This is not only understandable for Darwinists. A small child wants the gummy bears it has just seen now, immediately, rather than after the meal. Adults don't enjoy queuing in the cafeteria or at a checkout, but social convention keeps them from cutting the line. Those who were to do this, would be ostracized by the community and could expect collective aggression directed towards them. However, if the situation is rather anonymous, such as at an eBay auction or at the sales, then the inhibitions of the individual mostly disappear in order to reach their goal and beat others off the field. It is similar in a ritualized game: Sorry! is a good example.

But sometimes we behave not much differently in situations that are not as harmless as the bargain bin hunt or a board game: if the progress in the fast lane of the highway is too slow, this leads to tailgating and people flash their headlights in order to make the car in front of them clear the way. Inhibitions are low because the person is anonymized by the closed vehicle. But a car traveling 90 miles per hour covers 130 feet in one second, so we can easily calculate that if the person driving the vehicle in the front suddenly brakes there would be disastrous consequences. However, awareness of this has not reached those deep regions of the brain that affectively control our behavior. Our response time is adapted, as with "emotional" behavioral control, to the potential movements of the unprotected human body.

Handling music is not nearly as dangerous as handling motor vehicles. But the example illustrates that the evolution of our perception and emotional behavioral control often cannot keep up with cultural developments, especially not with the rapid advancement of technology. We must realize that the potential actions of the modern civilized person are not always supported or protected by his innate biological dispositions. This also applies to the area of communication: we can call each other in real time over large distances or communicate via Skype or e-mail. Theoretically, we could discuss by phone or e-mail every business query that was once discussed at the table. Nevertheless, business partners still get together for important meetings. Why? Because people do not only communicate with words, but through tone of voice and body language, and we include this information in our decisions.

Our perception of music and our emotional reactions to it are actually part of a behavioral repertoire in which musical expressions fulfill communicative functions, in which transmitter and receiver interact with each other. When we listen to music as a product and feel something, then we react to a situation in which we do not really find ourselves but that is indirectly represented and mapped: we are not standing in the midst of a crowd that is chanting for Barabbas to be released. However, listening to a CD of *St Matthew's Passion* we perceive this moment as such, and maybe even get one word.

This is nothing negative; it's the same with people that read a novel, look at a painting or watch a movie. But since music addresses uniquely direct and intense emotions, it can influence the emotions of the listener by simulating something.

For example, this emotional illusion is especially intense when a listener receives the stimulus of loud, rhythmic, percussive music. His body and mind react as if he himself is involved in the action, as if he himself is part of the group: a person would have experienced this stimuli in an "archaic" environment to which our perceptual system is adapted, a person would have experienced these stimuli only in the midst of drums and loud singing. However, our listener is on a train, he doesn't interact with the group; on the contrary, he is isolated from his real environment by earplugs. Music lets him plunge into an apparent community experience; in reality his behavior perpetuates loneliness.

The satisfaction provided by listening to music seems to make the more active, productive way of dealing with music increasingly unnecessary – even at the lantern parade on St Martin's Day. Cultural acceptance of this shift in the balance between active and passive music behavior has indeed existed before the invention of the record or since Adorno; the "listening" audience has been firmly established since the Baroque period. Thus the imbalance is stabilized and the laziness of people makes its own contribution.

But there are reasons that music educators, psychologists and doctors believe, when they point them out, that we would do well to develop and live out the skills of communication and expression that nature has given us. Whether one recognizes these good reasons in the development of one's personality, in the strengthening of social competence, in a commitment to cultural identity or simply in the joy of singing and making music, is up to each individual. We live in a modern industrial and information society and not in Plato's classical

Athens, so the challenge has to be rephrased: can we bring music more actively, productively and sensibly into the life of this society?

Let's look again in this context at "background music," now common practice in retail. Maybe it creates a pleasant acoustic background for the customers, maybe not. Nevertheless, department store music probably doesn't represent a particularly original attraction any longer – unless it is played live! I know of department stores in two large German cities that have their own grand piano. From time to time a pianist will sit there and play standards for an hour. The music fills the room, but it comes from a living source. One becomes curious, follows the music and finds the piano, maybe even lingers a while longer to listen to the end of the piece or to request a favorite song from the pianist. In any case, a real live background musician creates a much more personal atmosphere than a speaker. But even "canned music" one can deal with more consciously and discerningly, if you will.

Background music can be attractive when is introduced in doses and with a sense of where and when. However, a constant stream as a continuous ubiquitous state devalues music and does not do justice to our nature and perception. Music psychologists have long since pointed out that constantly playing similar pop music on the sales floor appeals to as many people as it drives away. A bit more interesting and potentially more effective advertising would be a program with different themes: Tuesday is jazz day, Thursday is classical day, and Friday is a day of silence. Maybe more customers that find background music annoying will then come on Fridays.

Where can "colloquial" singing and music-making now have their natural and authentic place outside of choirs, brass bands and amateur orchestras? Not everyone goes to church, but those who sometimes participate in worship are certainly familiar with the often unsatisfactory state of congregational singing. Almost everyone that sits in the pews knows the songs, but hardly anyone really sings along. Usually all you will heat are hesitant murmurs all around, though nothing stands in the way of trying out one's voice a little. You are allowed to be courageous outside of your shower! The organist always plays the hymns in one key, which everyone can sing along to – but please women, do not hum with the men!

To sing and make music, to live it as part of everyday culture and to introduce this to children means starting with the adults. When we arrange the equally loved and feared children's birthday parties, with balloons, chocolate-eating contests and treasure hunts, we often include "musical chairs" in the program or perhaps the "newspaper dance." These games are accompanied by music that is suddenly cut off at some point. One could simply insert a CD. But how would it be to make the music yourself? Some kind of instrument is available in almost every household, and if nobody plays the piano, guitar or flute, then maybe even a tambourine, or an harmonica that has been lying in a drawer for years, would suffice. Perhaps you can find a xylophone in the toy box and add that? The kitchen drawer can serve in an emergency as source of wooden percussion. Children don't expect perfection – and if they do expect it, then it is a good idea to show them alternatives. What is called for is improvisation and fun.

Those that grow up with the knowledge that making music is part of celebrating and living, will later have less inhibitions and fear of the unknown as teenagers and as adults, and be more inclined to act out musically: in a band, in a choir or in a private setting with their voice or with an instrument.

We have already mentioned the contemporary historical upheavals of music education in schools. But how is today's musical training of primary school teachers laid out? At Bavarian universities future teachers of primary and secondary schools study a scientific or artistic teaching subject and three other subjects as so-called didactic subjects, which means that they appoint didactic courses in these disciplines. Those who study music as a subject receive fairly extensive artistic training in singing, playing an instrument, in ensemble direction, rhythm, music theory and ear-training. Those who do not study music as their main subject – which is most of the students, because an artistic aptitude test is required in order to qualify – must choose one of their teaching subjects from music, art or sports. Up until now, students of music as a didactic subject received several semesters where they were taught singing and practical playing of the piano or guitar so that they were able to accompany songs in school. In the "modularized" teacher training program according to the Bologna Process, this minimal music study is to be further reduced in the future.

However, the majority of students that choose art or sport as their didactic subject don't receive any music education in their studies – but they still have to teach music in school (like almost all other subjects). Therefore there is a course for primary school teachers without musical training that they can attend for a few weekends in order to earn a "basic musical qualification." But even this course is no longer mandatory and no longer even offered for secondary school teachers.

Since one cannot learn musical practice from books, as opposed to local and general knowledge, we can understand the criticism that this system is ineffective for training teachers to provide lively, or even adequate, music education in primary and secondary school. Present regulations imply a devaluation of the subject compared to the previous training of teachers at pedagogical academies, which have been merged in the universities in most German states in the wake of the "scientification" of teacher training. At the former pedagogical universities the music program used to be a mandatory subject for the training of elementary school teachers – a status that the Ministers of Education must strive for again if they want to counteract "musical illiteracy" in children. But the political will to implement the advice of experts into action is not currently apparent.

But why do children need music at all? What good does it do? Let's leave the idealistic, educated middle position to consider music as an educational goal with intrinsic value, and list again the most important "end arguments" we have for pragmatists. One of the core targets of education is established almost as an afterthought when making music: self-activity. There is further scientific evidence that training for music-*making* (by which is meant both singing and playing an instrument) benefits cognitive performance and especially promotes social skills, thus the ability and willingness of children to get along with one another and accept the values of others. In general, we can certainly say, from an anthropological point of view, that music education promotes skills that belong to the nature, to the "basic equipment", of men, such as movement, language skills or logical reasoning.

So, "an instrument for every child" (as is being promoted in Germany's Ruhr area)? The idea sounds impressive, but it would be even simpler and easier to implement "ten songs for each child." Singing is the immediate, primary form of musical expression, before the use of "tools," a behavior that creates an emotional bond in all cultures and forms community. Theodor Adorno saw the negative side of this phenomenon, but the positive is just as obvious. Does it matter which songs our children learn? Not especially, since the cultural structure in which we live is also supported by historical pillars. Traditional folk songs are those that appeal to archetypal motifs, which raise awareness of cultural roots, and these are the songs which children can sing with their grandparents. There are good reasons to give the folk song a place of honor in music education, also on an intellectual level. Adorno claimed, not incorrectly, that children should learn to understand pieces of art in music class, rather than singing mindlessly. Had he overlooked the fact that the "high" art music of the last three centuries has been permeated with folk music and that important composers have repeatedly processed and revived folk songs, folk dances and church songs? "folk style" does not only play a central role in romantics such as Schubert, Schumann and Brahms. It is also the nucleus of the symphonic works of Gustav Mahler, who evoked the folk traditions in order to represent a more dismaying sense of the upheaval at the turn of the century – an artistic statement that would not be understood without this background of "naiveté." In modern times it is mainly Bela Bartók and Paul Hindemith that implement folk songs in their compositions. Thus the familiarity with folk songs and folk music heritage is a prerequisite for the understanding of "classical" and modern art of music.

"I'm not musical" – one often hears this self-assessment from people. But is it justifiable?

Must every person be able to do something with music, and must we educate every child about music or with music? Many people are convinced that they have no musical talent. In particular, when it comes to singing many often say, with a certain irony, that they would rather not expose the environment to their off-key voice.

Everyone is undoubtedly not equally gifted: some "have it," others do not. One must realistically recognize that not everyone can paint like Franz Marc and it is probably not a good idea to make the entire population participate in the Athletics Championships or study for a PhD in mathematics. Above all, we often perceive music as a concert-goer or through the media only as a stream of exceptional talent, whose ability is beyond reach for the layman. The image of the highly talented, often eccentric virtuoso (from Farinelli to Paganini, up to Lang Lang) has characterized the music scene since the Baroque period. Musicians are, so it seems, special people who received the talent in the cradle. Ever since the seven-year-old Wolfgang Amadeus Mozart was presented by his father throughout Europe as a child prodigy, the idea that a gifted musician will be noticed in his early childhood has spread.

But if music educators, developmental psychologists and physicians advertise singing and music-making to the population, then they are not concerned with high artistic achievement. Their aim is for us to use and develop the potential with which each and every one of us is equipped by nature "as standard." Our brain, our vocal apparatus and our hearing are built in such a way so that we not only express ourselves and communicate in words, but also in tones. We are musical by nature and we are equipped to recognize a melody and repeat it, to perceive a rhythm and tap to the beat and to modulate the voice beyond the talking range.

Just as we expect any healthy child to be able to read, write, calculate and ride a bike, so we can also expect them to have musical skills. But those skills can only unfold when they are encouraged and unhindered. The self-assessment "I'm not musical" or "I can't sing" relates back to negative experiences during childhood in most cases. If a child is told in school, "You don't sing properly," they are discouraged, the latent embarrassment runs rampant and they fall silent. Children who sing incorrectly or off key in a group are for the most part just musically untrained and feel insecure.

There is however a small, although not negligible, part of the population with an innate, genetic musical deficit, about three per cent. These people lack the ability of relative hearing, which means that they cannot recognize and repeat a song, even with practice. The ability to talk and even to feel rhythm is usually not affected, which is why one can hardly call congenital amusia a "disorder," as it does not affect life in any other area. Those who want to find out whether they belong to this minority can take a test that was specially developed for the detection of amusia.[2]

Good Paths

What is the "political" demand for a conscious, active approach to music ultimately about? Initially, it is about better understanding what music really means to people – about seeing the mosaic as a whole, which is composed of scientific knowledge that is mostly published only as individual articles in scientific journals and therefore often remain hidden from the wider public. Let us formulate the essence once more.

In addition to language that allows us humans to specifically name things, the evolution of our species has created another communication system – simultaneously to or perhaps even before language – that is based on rhythm and melody. There must have been a good "biological" reason for the development of the capabilities to recognize melody and rhythm and to use them as a means of expression and communication – just as there was probably just as good a reason for the evolution of other complex cognitive abilities and behavioral characteristics. All the recognizable evolutionary causes of human musicality have to do with an emotional bond, with the "social glue" that is vital to *Homo sapiens* as a social being. This anthropological knowledge does not contradict the cultural, historical or aesthetic consideration of music as an art or a lust-provoking activity. Rather, it highlights another level. Knowledge of these connections gives rise to the demand for a higher significance – or rather for new self-evidence – that singing and music-making is beneficial to society, especially in parenting and educational work. Studies in evolutionary anthropology, ethology, the effects of music, but also European cultural history, of the relationship between the condition of a society and its approach to music teach us that musical behavior is a part of the *conditio humana*, it belongs to the nature of social man. To cut down on music education, to devalue music to mere sound, but also to stylize it into a pure luxury item would be a risky gamble with the future of our culture. Music creates identity. It is not only to be understood as a remedy in a medical sense, but primarily as a remedy for the alienation of man from himself.

However, to only complain about flaws and put forward demands would leave a distorted image of our musical culture. In the introduction of this book we encountered three episodes of singing and music-making in an equally surprising and everyday way: as an activity of our ancestors from 30,000 years ago, as a hobby by which a cellular phone salesman suddenly becomes world-famous and as the key to unlock the lost memories of an old lady.

This expedition should end now with some examples of musical activity that have a certain model character. All three examples concern a self-evident and conscious use of music as a part of life. Music plays a large part in creating an ideal home for the individual and in strengthening social relationships between people in all three examples. Apparent boundaries between art and everyday life disappear in all three examples.

The Neubeuern choral society is well-known in the international concert landscape. Under the direction of their conductor Enoch zu Guttenberg, the choral society mostly performs together with the Munich KlangVerwaltung, a project orchestra that is composed of members of leading symphony and opera orchestras.

Their repertoire mainly includes that of the great oratorios of music history: the *Christmas Oratorio* and the *Passions* by Johann Sebastian Bach, Joseph Haydn's *Creation*, the highly emotional requiem setting of the composer Giuseppe Verdi and many other musically and technically demanding choral works. The Neubeuern not only performs in the great concert halls of Munich, but also in the Berlin Philharmonic, the traditional Viennese musical society and the Concertgebouw in Amsterdam. In 2009, they went on tour in China.

A globally active concert choir like so many others? This is partially true, but both the history of the choir as well as its conception of music is exceptional. In 1967, young music student Enoch zu Guttenberg took over the choral society in the small Upper Bavarian village of Neubeuern, which is located in the Inn Valley. With the term "choral society" one associates, not unduly, a simple down-to-earth repertoire. However, Guttenberg and the Neubeuern choir expanded this repertoire in a very short time and sang sets of Buxtehude and Bach at their first Advent caroling. Two years later, they held their first performance in the Munich Theatinerkirche, featuring works by Vivaldi, Bach and Handel. The criticism was impressive and the step up to *St Matthew's Passion* and to the stages of great concert halls was soon accomplished.

How was this advancement possible? One answer is through the suggestive power and passion of the conductor. The other answer is the established musical potential on-site. From time immemorial a lively music tradition (i.e., folk music), passed down through generations without academic music education, has been exercised in different forms in Neubeuern and its surroundings. That is why it so happens that many singers of the choir have learned the oratorios of Bach and Haydn without being able to accurately read notes (and we even know that some of the most famous jazz musicians can do without this written help). The system of singing along with repetition works because the brain does not store music by reading, but by listening and doing. The Neubeuern choir represents all occupational groups. As all choir members were previously from Neubeuern or the surrounding villages, there were many farmers and artisans among the singers due to the (then) relatively rural structure of the population. This earned the Neubeuern choir the label "peasant choir" in the press – which reflects a slightly distorted perspective of a music industry that would basically attribute high art only to urban culture.

However, the Neubeuern choir is living proof of the seamless connection between folk music and so-called art music, especially because it has never contemptuously discarded popular music. Each year in December, Enoch zu Guttenberg and his choir perform sets of Alpine Christmas songs, three-part singing and string music. A few days later, the program features Bach's *Christmas Oratorio*.

Now, if one looks at the rows of singers, one need not look far to find young faces. Unlike some other amateur choirs, the Neubeuern choir hardly has any recruitment problems. Many of the young members are children of choir singers; several families are represented in the choir by two or even three generations. Once there is a certain number of young people singing in a choir, then their friends join too – and how many teenagers have the chance to not only witness a big concert with internationally renowned singers and instrumentalists in a world class venue, but also to participate? To participate actively in the chorus, one must of course meet some requirements – not just anyone can sing the *Christmas Oratorio* in the Munich Philharmonic concert hall. That is why children are prepared for the choir society by attending a youth choir and having vocal training lessons.

Guttenberg does not only care about beauty, about *l'art pour l'art*. He does not make music in order to convey sounds; he makes music to convey content. In an oratorio it's mainly religious belief, in a folk song it can be devotion or an overwhelming love of life. "The simple songs are the hardest," says Guttenberg, referring to the lost innocence of the people in our society, the uncertainty and skepticism in regards to the cultural homeland we basically long for.

In 2003, the Berlin Philharmonic, their chief conductor Sir Simon Rattle and the dance teacher Royston Maldoom created a connection between bourgeois high culture and its seemingly opposite sphere. They rehearsed the choreography of the ballet *The Rite of Spring* by Igor Stravinsky with 250 children and adolescents from twenty-five nations. Most of the young people attended primary schools in the so-called "deprived" areas of Berlin, which had previously hardly ever come into contact with classical music. Nevertheless, it was possible to bring the project to a performance level within six weeks – which was as great a success, as its accompanying documentary *Rhythm Is It!* "When the people do not come to the orchestra then the orchestra goes to the people," says Simon Rattle. The choreographer, Maldoom, who had previously completed dance projects with street children and detainees, inspired the students by demanding discipline and concentration and by showing the adolescents that he trusts them to accomplish something. Maldoom explains,

> I always demand what makes the piece, the dance, the best. That's the whole secret. I do not care where the children come from and what else is going on in their lives; they also don't want to be reminded of that. They want something new and exciting. And the dance is exciting. That is where social relations start, mainly depending on what the choreography demands. And that is what gives children relief from their problems. They have to risk something and have to accomplish something, which they do, and they can even do it really well, and thus they create a new image of themselves: Wow, I can do this, I'm much better at it than I thought.[3]

The documentary follows three students whose lives are changed by the work of *The Rite of Spring*, who are enthralled, who challenge themselves, who take responsibility and find their way out of isolation. Dance holds people together, says Maldoom. It helps people to experience the feeling of being part of the group, to support each other and to develop more empathy for each other and for the teacher.

One does not necessarily need a world-class orchestra such as the Berlin Philharmonic to get young people off the street and onto the stage. Since 2000, special education teacher Susanne Korbmacher, together with the club Ghettokids (which she cofounded) in the infamous Munich settlement Hasenbergl, organizes social and creative projects for the youth of the district. The young participants involved in the theater, singing projects and drum groups are in "real life" students of the local special educational center: they have severe learning difficulties, display behavioral problems, their social and family backgrounds are often disastrous and only a few of them are children of German parents. The name Ghettokids is no accident. However, the situation is not hopeless.

When a teenager finds his way into a theater or rap group and says, "This is cooler than the street," then Korbmacher feels she has passed the first hurdle. Just like Maldoom, she knows that those who learn productive cooperation in a band or on stage and can "blow off steam", will very rarely assault someone later that day. These successeses verify Korbmacher's opinions, and many "Ghettokids" have later managed to finish school and acquire an apprenticeship. The creative projects entice them to take on responsibility, to demand something of themselves and to break away from their seemingly predetermined destiny of living on the street and in jail.

Maybe the foundations of social behavior could be oriented early on for most children, so that they do not end up as social outcasts later. It has already been said that an improvement in music education in primary school can contribute to this, and also that the conditions for more effective teacher training and lesson plans need to be created. However, music education – in terms of upbringing and education through music – begins even earlier. The opinions about Waldorf education differ, and perhaps Steiner schools are not suited for every child and teenager. But the concept of the Waldorf kindergarten is of some help to the nature-friendly development of preschoolers. This educational work takes advantage of the great receptiveness of young children and their desire for imitation: "The result is a basic educational task for adults: the direct environment of the child must be designed in such a way that it is worthy of being imitated."[4]

The key element to this educational environment is rhythm: a strong connection to nature, seasons and festive days, a structured weekly schedule (every day of the week has its own "breakfast cereal") and a fixed structure of the day. Short rhymes and songs are introduced to accompany activities of the daily routine. The reliable recurrences of these small rituals give the child an inner feeling of safety: it knows what to do. Late midmorning the teacher announces the end of the free playing time by singing a rhyme:

> Clean up time, clean up time,
> clean up time is here!

That is the signal for the children to put the toys back in boxes and baskets. The playing material includes large colored sheets that need to be folded together again. With the help of adults, the children learn how to do this: two children take a sheet, holding two corners. First the sheet is thrown up, creating a wave and then the children approach each other while placing the corners together. Then the whole procedure repeats itself with the sheet folded in half. All the while the teachers sing with the children:

> We rock,
> we rock

> little angels
> up into heaven!

Before "heaven" the children have to create momentum so that a beautiful wave is formed, which for toddlers is not an easy task to synchronize. Even washing your hands before eating is accompanied by a song that makes the chore into a game. When all the children are sitting at the table with the teachers they sing together:

> The birds fly high into the sky and far into the world,
> just as it pleases them,
> and home to their nest
> to steady themselves.

The lyrics are simultaneously represented by movement. At "home to their nest" the children form a nest with their hands, at "steady themselves" they place their hands together so that the song leads up to a short grace.

After lunch and once the dishes are cleared silence sets in once again as the teacher reads a story to all the children at the end of the morning. This is initiated by ringing a bell and the teacher sings:

> Quiet, quiet, listen up!
> What does it mean?
> If you have good ears,
> you will hear something ringing.

The children sit in a circle on the floor and listen to a story that rings out the end of the day in kindergarten. They perceive singing as a natural and meaningful part of life, just as the romantic Joseph von Eichendorff implored:

> Schläft ein Lied in allen Dingen
> die da träumen fort und fort,
> und die Welt hebt an zu singen,
> triffst du nur das Zauberwort.[5]

NOTES

Prelude

1 "You're lucky with the Ladies, Bel Ami'", a German hit from the 1930s.
2 *Eiszeit. Kunst und Kultur.* Companion volume to state exhibition. Baden-Württemberg 2009. Ostfildern 2009.
3 Claudius Conrad, *Requiem oder Ouvertüre – Physiologische Effekte durch Mozartsche Klaviersonaten bei schwerstkranken Intensivpatienten.* Dissertation, University of Munich, 2006.
4 See Iain Morley, "Evolution of the Physiological and Neurological Capacities for Music," *Cambridge Archaeological Journal* 12 (2002): 195–216.
5 Klaus Wachsmann, *Essays on Music and History in Africa* (Evanston, IL: Northwestern University Press, 1971).
6 See for example Marcel Zentner and Jerome Kagan, "Infants Perception of Consonance and Dissonance in Music," *Infant Behavior and Development* 21 (1998): 483–92; as well as diverse studies by psychologist Sandra Trehub.

Chapter 1: Musical Nature

1 Ovid, *Metamorphoses* I, 689ff., translation by Sir Samuel Garth, John Dryden, et al.
2 Jean-Jacques Rousseau, "Essai sur l'origine des langues où il est parlé de la mélodie et de l'imitation musicale" (1762).
3 Heinrich Heine, *Letters from Berlin*, second letter, 16 March 1822 (Frankfurt, 1991).
4 Charles Darwin, *The Descent of Man and Selection in Relation to Sex* (London, 1871).
5 See for example, opinion on creationism by the Protestant Center for Religious and Ideological Issues in EKD, "Dem Kreationismus argumentativ begegnen," 23 July 2007, online: http://www.ekd.de/aktuell_presse/pm67_2007_ezw_schoepfungsglaube.html (accessed 9 September 2013); scientific conference "Biological Evolution: Facts and Theories" at the Pontifical University Gregorian, Rome 2009, online: http://www.evolution-rome2009.net (accessed 9 September 2013); Christian conception of man and evolution theories: message of Pope John Paul II to the members of the Pontifical Academy of Sciences in regards to their plenary assembly on 22 October 1996.
6 Canon, attributed to Wolfgang Amadeus Mozart.
   Translation:
   Everything is silent, nightingales
   Lure with sweet melodies
   Tears in the eye, sadness in the heart.
7 Latin word game of unknown origin: "The lark praises the Lord when it rises into the heavens."

8   Olivier Messiaen, talk given at the World Exposition 1958 in Brussels.
9   Peter Marler, "Origins of Music and Speech," in *The Origins of Music*, ed. Wallin, Nils, Merker, Björn, Brown, Steven (Cambridge, MA, 2000), 31–48.
10 See Patricia M. Gray et al., "The Music of Nature and the Nature of Music," *Science* 291 (2001): 52–4.
11 J.R. Krebs, "Song and Territory in the Great Tit *Parus major*," in *Evolutionary Ecology* (London, 1977), 47–62.
12 Seth Coleman, "Female Preferences Drive the Evolution of Mimetic Accuracy in Male Sexual Displays," *Biology Letters* 3 (2007): 463–6.
13 Bernhard Hoffmann, *Kunst und Vogelgesang* (Leipzig, 1908).
14 William T. Fitch, "The Evolution of Music in Comparative Perspective," *Cognition* 100 (2006), 173–215.
15 Only a few people have so-called "perfect pitch."
16 Josh McDermott and Marc Hauser, "The Evolution of the Music Faculty: A Comparative Perspective," *Nature Neuroscience* 6:7 (2003): 663–8. Psychologists have conducted several relevant studies where almost all showed that the studied species doesn't have relative pitch. An exception is the study by Wright et al. from the year 2000. According to this study, rhesus monkeys hear the so-called octave generalization (i.e., they recognize two short melodies that sound in succession in one octave as the same), but only when it comes to tunes from the diatonic scale.
17 Of course one can only refer to amusia as a "disorder" if it is perceived as such by the person in question.
18 "Hurray, the whole town is here!"
19 Reinhard Kopiez and Guido Brink, *Fußball-Fangesänge. Eine FANomenologie* (Würzburg, 1999).
20 "All My Little Ducklings are Swimming in the Lake."
21 Ibid.
22 Aniruddh D. Patel, "Musical Rhythm, Linguistic Rhythm, and Human Evolution," *Music Perception* 24 (2006): 99–104.
23 Ibid.
24 By vocal tract one refers to the organs that are directly involved in voice production: i.e., trachea, larynx (and therein the vocal cords or vocal folds), pharynx and oral cavity.
25 Mario Vaneechoutte and John Skoyles, "The Memetic Origin of Language: Modern Humans as Musical Primates," *Journal of Memetics: Evolutionary Models of Information Transmission* 2 (1998).
26 Darwin, *The Descent of Man*.
27 Clifford Geertz, Thick Description: Toward an Interpretive Theory of Culture. In *The Interpretation of Culture* (New York, 1973).
28 Darwin, *The Descent of Man*.
29 Steven Pinker, *How the Mind Works* (New York, 1997), 528.
30 For the universality of the lullaby, refer to the studies by Canadian psychologist Sandra Trehub.
31 Dean Falk, "The 'Putting the Baby Down' Hypothesis: Bipedalism, Babbling, and Baby Slings," *Behavioral and Brain Sciences* 27 (2004): 526–34.

32 Under the description of *Homo erectus* (the upright man), anthropologists summarize a number of different fossil finds together into a stage of development from which both "modern" man as well as Neanderthals emerged. *Homo erectus* mastered the fire and made specialized stone tools.
33 See Jean Liedloff, *The Continuum Concept. In Search of Happiness Lost* (London, 1975). Other exemplary names would be Mechthild Papousek in Germany and Sandra Trehub in Canada.
34 Edward Hagen and Gregory Bryant, "Music and Dance as a Coalition Signaling system," *Human Nature* 14 (2003): 21–51.
35 Karl Bücher was the first to formulate this relationship in his writing, *Arbeit und Rhythmus* (1899).
36 Robin I. Dunbar, "The Origin and Subsequent Evolution of Language," in *Language Evolution*, ed. M.H. Christiansen and S. Kirby (Oxford, 2003), 219–34.
37 Jaak Panksepp and Günther Bernatzky, "Emotional Sounds and the Brain: The Neuro-Affective Foundations of Musical Appreciation," *Behavioral Processes* 60 (2002): 133–55; Oliver Grewe et al., "Listening to Music as a Re-creative Process: Physiological, Psychological and Psychoacoustical Correlations of Chills and Strong Emotions," *Music Perception* 23 (2007): 297–314.
38 Fitch, "The Evolution of Music."
39 John Tooby and Leda Cosmides, Does Beauty Build Adapted Minds? Toward an Evolutionary Theory of Aesthetics, Fiction and the Arts. *SubStance* 94/95 (2001): 6–27.
40 The principle of "preservation of the species" in older evolutionary biology and ethology was later dropped. Meanwhile, however, the theory of "group selection" experienced a certain renaissance.
41 Latin, *proximus* – next one.
42 Latin, *ultimus* – last one.
43 "Fine new potatoes from Neuburg on the Danube.".
44 Otto Böckel, *Psychologie der Volksdichtung* (Leipzig, 1906).
45 Christian Lehmann, *Singstreit, Ständchen und Signale* (Berlin, 2009).
46 Knud Rasmussen, *Der Sängerkrieg. Eskimosagen aus Grönland* (1922, repr.: Berlin, 1991), 234.
47 Desmond Morris, "Typical Intensity and Its Relationship to the Problems of Ritualization," *Behavior* 11 (1956): 1–12.
48 Wulf Schiefenhövel and Jörg Blumtritt,"Kommunikation – eine Einführung" in *Brockhaus Mensch, Natur, Technik: Phänomen Mensch* (Leipzig, 1999).
49 Steven Brown, "The 'Musilanguage' Model of Music Evolution," in *The Origins of Music*, ed. Nils Wallin, Björn Merker, Steven Brown (Cambridge, MA, 2000), 271–300.

Chapter 2: Musical Culture

1 Curt Sachs, *Geist und Werden der Musikinstrumente* (Berlin 1929), 63.
2 Nicholas Conard, Die Anfänge der Musik. Eine Knochenflöte aus dem unteren Aurignacien, in *Eiszeit. Kunst und Kultur*, ed. Württembergisches Landesmuseum (Stuttgart 2009)

3 The use of the term "Stone Age" in the context of contemporary societies (such as in Africa, New Guinea, South America, etc.) is occasionally attacked. However, the term is justified as it literally refers to cultures that use stone tools, don't know of metal extraction and have not developed script – similar to the Central European state of civilization of more than 5,000 years ago. Globalization processes have certainly rapidly and dramatically changed the ways of life of these societies in recent decades.
4 Plato, *Protagoras* 326a–b, translated by Benjamin Jowett. http://classics.mit.edu/Plato/protagoras.html (accessed Oct 27, 2013).
5 Plato, *The Republic* 398d–399a. Plato in Twelve Volumes, Vols. 5 & 6 translated by Paul Shorey. (Cambridge, MA; London, 1969).
6 Joachim Ernst Berendt, *Nada Brahma – Die Welt ist Klang* (Frankfurt, 1983).
7 Some acousticians guide the perception of consonances back to "subharmonics" complemented by the auditory system.
8 The psychologist Carl Stumpf performed these studies toward the end of the nineteenth century.
9 Arnold Schönberg, *Harmonielehre* (Vienna, 1922).
10 Plato, *The Republic* 424c. Plato in Twelve Volumes, Vols. 5 & 6 translated by Paul Shorey. (Cambridge, MA; London, 1969).
11 Steven Pinker, *How the Mind Works*.
12 Max Wegner, *Musikgeschichte in Bildern: Griechenland* (Leipzig, 1963), 84.
13 Aristotle, *Politics*, Book VIII.
14 *Liber argumentorum: Expositiones in micrologum guidonis aritini*, ed. J. Smits van Waesberghe (Amsterdam, 1957).
15 Sebastian Franck, *Weltbuch* (1534)
16 Benedetto Marcello, *Il teatro alla moda* (1720), quoted in Romain Goldron, *Illustrierte Geschichte der Musik Vol. 5* (Lausanne, 1966), 84.
17 Maurice Andrieux, *La vie dans la Rome pontificale au XVIIIe siècle*, quoted in Romain Goldron (1966), 85f.
18 Johann Nikolaus Forkel, *Genauere Bestimmung einiger musikalischer Begriffe zur Ankündigung des akademischen Winter-Concerts von Michaelis 1780 bis Ostern 1781* (Göttingen, 1780).
19 Heinrich Christoph Koch, *Musicalisches Lexikon* (Frankfurt, 1802).
20 Eduard Hanslick, *Geschichte des Konzertwesens in Wien* (Vienna, 1869), ix.
21 Eduard Hanslick, *Vom Musikalisch-Schönen* (Leipzig, 1854).
22 Ibid.
23 Wilhelm Feldmann, 1830, quoted in Walter Salmen, *Musikgeschichte in Bildern Vol. IV, No. 3: Haus- und Kammermusik* (Leipzig, 1969).
24 Adolph Bernhard Marx, *Die Musik des neunzehnten Jahrhunderts und ihre Pflege: Methode der Musik* (Leipzig, 1855), 130.
25 Robert Schumann, quoted in Walter Salmen, 1969.
26 Dietrich Fischer-Dieskau, *Auf den Spuren der Schubert-Lieder* (Munich, 1976).
27 Max Friedlaender, *Das deutsche Lied, Vol. 1.1* (Berlin, 1902), xii.
28 Silcher's own comments in his manuscript.
29 Kurt Pahlen, *Die große Geschichte der Musik* (Berlin, 2002).
30 *Scientific American*, Dec 22, 1877.
31 Pahlen 2002.

Chapter 3: Music and Person

1. Sloboda (1991); Panksepp and Bernatzky (2002), Grewe et al. (2007).
2. Erin Hannon and Glenn Schellenberg, "Early Development of Music and Language," in *Music Psychology: The New Handbook*, ed. Herbert Bruhn et al. (Hamburg, 2008), 131–43.
3. Jayne Standley, "A Meta-analysis of the Efficacy of Music Therapy for Premature Infants," *Journal of Pediatric Nursing* 17, no. 2 (2002): 107–13.
4. Sandra Trehub et al., "Mothers and Fathers Singing to Infants," *Developmental Psychology* 33 (1997): 500–507.
5. Gunter Kreutz et al., "Effects of Choir Singing or Listening on Secretory Immunoglobulin A, Cortisol and Emotional state," *Journal of Behavioral Medicine* 27 (2004): 623–35.
6. 1 Samuel 16:14–23.
7. Hidehiko Okamoto et al., "Listening to Tailor-Made Notched Music Reduces Tinnitus Loudness and Tinnitus-Related Auditory Cortex Activity," *Proceedings of the National Academy of Sciences* (2009). Online: http://www.pnas.org/cgi/doi/10.1073/pnas.0911268107 (accessed 16th September 2013).
8. Herbert Bruhn and Eva-Maria Franck-Bleckwedel, "Rezeptive Musiktherapy," in *Musikpsychologie. Ein Handbuch*, ed. Herbert Bruhn et al. (Reinbek, 1993).
9. Tonius Timmermann, "Rezeptive und aktive Musiktherapy in der Praxis" in *Die Heilkraft der Musik. Einführung in die Musiktherapie*, ed. Werner Kraus (Munich, 1998).
10. Kassel Theses on Music Therapy.
11. Christine Plahl, "Musiktherapie – Praxisfelder und Vorgehensweisen" in *Musikpsychologie. Ein Handbuch*, ed. Herbert Bruhn et al. (Reinbek, 1993).12 See Christian Lehmann, *Singstreit, Ständchen und Signale: Zur Biologie und Evolution musikalischen Verhaltens* (Berlin, 2009).
13. See Dieter E. Zimmer, *Tiefenschwindel. Die endlose und die beendbare Psychoanalyse* (Reinbek, 1986).
14. Cesar Bresgen, *Musik-Erziehung? Ein kritisches Protokoll* (Wilhelmshaven 1975): 39.
15. Hans Günther Bastian, *Kinder optimal fördern – mit Musik* (Mainz 2001): 29.
16. See http://www.karladamek.de (accessed 16th September 2013); and Andreas Göpfert, "Chorleiter-Weiterbildung: Auf ein Neues," in *Neue Musikzeitung* 3 (2003).
17. Karl Adamek and especially Andreas Mohr provide detailed information on the theme on their websites: http://www.karladamek.de and http://www.kinderstimmbildung.de (accessed 16th September 2013).
18. Theodor W. Adorno, "Kritik des Musikanten" in *Dissonanzen* (Göttingen, 1956).
19. Michael Alt, *Didaktik der Musik* (Düsseldorf, 1968).
20. Helmut Segler, "Macht Singen dumm?" *Westermanns Pädagogische Beiträge* 3 (1976): 139ff.
21. Margrit Küntzel-Hansen, *Die Liederkommode* (Velber, 1973).
22. Jochen Unbehaun, *Musikunterricht. Alternative Modelle* (Bensheim, 1980).

Chapter 4: Risk More Music

1. Geertz, Clifford. Thick Description. Toward an Interpretive Theory of Culture. In *The Interpretation of Culture* (New York, 1973).

2 Amusia Online Test, Isabella Peretz Research Laboratory, University of Montreal. Online: http://www.brams.umontreal.ca/amusia-general (accessed 17th September 2013).
3 Interview with Royston Maldoom, *Spiegel Online*, 18th November 2008. Online: http://www.spiegel.de/spiegelspecial/a-590829.html (accessed 17th September 2013).
4 Waldorfkindergartenseminar, "Was kleine Kinder brauchen – Vom Ansatz der Waldorfpädagogik." Online: http://www.waldorfkindergartenseminar.de (accessed 17th September 2013).
5 Sleeps a song in all things,
That dream on and on,
And the world begins to sing,
If only you find the magic word.

BIBLIOGRAPHY

Alt, Michael. *Didaktik der Musik* (Düsseldorf, 1968).
Archäologisches Landesmuseum Baden-Württemberg and Department Ältere Urgeschichte und Quartärökologie, Eberhard Karls Universität Tübingen (Hrsg.): *Eiszeit. Kunst und Kultur*. Companion volume to Große Landesausstellung Baden-Württemberg 2009. Ostfildern 2009
Aristotle. *Politik*. Translated and edited by Olof Gigon. Munich, 1984.
Bastian, Hans Günther. *Kinder optimal fördern – mit Musik* (Mainz 2001): 29.
Berendt, Joachim Ernst. *Nada Brahma: Die Welt ist Klang*. Frankfurt, 1983.
Böckel, Otto. *Psychologie der Volksdichtung*. Leipzig, 1906.
Bresgen, Cesar. *Musik-Erziehung? Ein kritisches Protokoll* (Wilhelmshaven, 1975)
Brown, Steven. "The 'Musilanguage' Model of Music Evolution." In *The Origins of Music*, edited by Nils Wallin, Björn Merker and Steven Brown. Cambridge, MA, 2000, 271–300.
Bruhn, Herbert, Rolf Oerter and Helmut Rösing, eds. *Musikpsychologie. Ein Handbuch*. Reinbek, 1993.
Bruhn, Herbert, Reinhard Kopiez and Andreas C. Lehmann, eds. *Musikpsychologie. Das neue Handbuch*. Reinbek, 2008.
Brünger, Peter. *Singen im Kindergarten. Untersuchung unter bayerischen und niedersächsischen Kindergartenfachkräften*. Augsburg, 2003.
Bücher, Karl. *Arbeit und Rhythmus*. Leipzig, 1899.
Coleman, Seth. "Female Preferences Drive the Evolution of Mimetic Accuracy in Male Sexual Displays." *Biology Letters* 3 (2007), 463–6.
Conrad, Claudius. *Requiem oder Ouvertüre – Physiologische Effekte durch Mozartsche Klaviersonaten bei schwerstkranken Intensivpatienten*. Dissertation, University of Munich, 2006.
Darwin, Charles. *The Descent of Man and Selection in Relation to Sex*. London, 1871.
———. *The Expression of Emotions in Man and Animal*. London, 1872.
Dunbar, Robin I. "The Origin and Subsequent Evolution of Language." In *Language Evolution*, edited by M.H Christiansen and S. Kirby, 219–34. Oxford, 2003.
Eibl, Karl. *Animal Poeta: Bausteine der biologischen Kultur- und Literaturtheorie*. Paderborn, 2004.
Eibl-Eibesfeldt, Irenäus. *Die Biologie des menschlichen Verhaltens*. Munich, 1986.
Eibl-Eibesfeldt, Irenäus and Christa Sütterlin. *Weltsprache Kunst. Zur Natur- und Kunstgeschichte bildlicher Kommunikation*. Vienna, 2008.
Falk, Dean. "The 'Putting the Baby Down' Hypothesis: Bipedalism, Babbling, and Baby Slings." *Behavioral and Brain Sciences* 27 (2004): 526–34.
Finscher, Ludwig, ed. *Die Musik in Geschichte und Gegenwart*. Kassel/Stuttgart, 1994–2007.
Fischer-Dieskau, Dietrich. *Auf den Spuren der Schubert-Lieder*. Munich, 1976.

Fitch, William T. "The Evolution of Music in Comparative Perspective." *Cognition* 100 (2006): 173–215.
Forkel, Johann Nikolaus. *Genauere Bestimmung einiger musikalischer Begriffe zur Ankündigung des akademischen Winter-Concerts von Michaelis 1780 bis Ostern 1781.* Göttingen, 1780.
Franck, Sebastian. *Weltbuch* (1534).
Friedlaender, Max. *Das deutsche Lied.* Vol. 1.1. Berlin, 1902.
Geertz, Clifford. "Thick Description. Toward an Interpretive Theory of Culture." In *The Interpretation of Culture* (New York, 1973).
Göpfert, Andreas. "Chorleiter-Weiterbildung: Auf ein Neues." In *Neue Musikzeitung* 3 (2003).
Gray, Patricia M. et al. "The Music of Nature and the Nature of Music." *Science* 291 (2001): 52–4.
Grewe, Oliver et al. "Listening to Music as a Re-creative Process: Physiological, Psychological and Psychoacoustical Correlations of Chills and Strong Emotions." *Music Perception* 23 (2007): 297–314.
Hagen, Edward and Gregory Bryant. "Music and Dance as a Coalition Signaling System." *Human Nature* 14 (2003), 21–51.
Hanslick, Eduard. *Vom Musikalisch-Schönen.* Leipzig, 1854.
_____. *Geschichte des Konzertwesens in Wien.* Vienna, 1869.
Heine, Heinrich. *Letters from Berlin*, second letter, 16 March 1822 (Frankfurt, 1991).
Hoffmann, Bernhard. *Kunst und Vogelgesang.* Leipzig, 1908.
Hornbostel, Erich Moritz von. *Tonart und Ethos. Aufsätze zur Musikethnologie und Musikpsychologie*, edited by Christian Kaden and Erich Stockmann. Leipzig, 1986.
Koch, Heinrich Christoph. *Musicalisches Lexikon.* Frankfurt, 1802.
Kopiez, Reinhard and Guido Brink. *Fußball-Fangesänge. Eine FANomenologie.* Würzburg, 1999.
Krebs, J.R. "Song and Territory in the Great Tit *Parus major.*" In *Evolutionary Ecology* (London, 1977): 47–62.
Kreutz, Gunter et al. "Effects of Choir Singing or Listening on Secretory Immunoglobulin A, Cortisol and Emotional State." *Journal of Behavioral Medicine* 27 (2004): 623–35.
Küntzel-Hansen, Margrit. *Die Liederkommode* (Velber, 1973).
Lehmann, Christian. "Gesang als Signal. Humanethologische Aspekte des Singens" In *Stimmkulturen. Kinder- und Jugendstimme*, Vol. 2, edited by M. Fuchs, 9–21. Leipzig, 2007.
_____. *Singstreit, Ständchen und Signale: Zur Biologie und Evolution musikalischen Verhaltens.* Berlin, 2009.
Lehmann, Christian, Lorenz Welker and Wulf Schiefenhövel. "Towards an Ethology of Song: A Categorization of Musical Behavior." Special issue, *Musicae Scientiae* (2009–10): 321–38.
Liedloff, Jean. *The Continuum Concept. In Search of Happiness Lost* (London, 1975).
Lorenz, Konrad. *Das sogenannte Böse.* Munich, 1963.
Marcello, Benedetto. *Il teatro alla moda* (1720). Quoted in: Romain Goldron. *Illustrierte Geschichte der Musik Vol. 5.* Lausanne, 1966.
Marx, Adolph Bernhard. *Die Musik des neunzehnten Jahrhunderts und ihre Pflege: Methode der Musik.* Leipzig, 1855.

BIBLIOGRAPHY 153

Mathelitsch, Leopold and Friedrich, Gerhard. *Die Stimme*. Berlin, 1995.
Mawick, Reinhard. "Singen. Vom Segen des Singens" In *Chrismon*, an insert in the *Frankfurter Rundschau* 9 (2002).
McDermott, Josh and Marc Hauser. "The Evolution of the Music Faculty: A Comparative Perspective." *Nature Neuroscience* 6, no. 7 (2003): 663–8.
McNeill, William H. *Keeping Together in Time: Dance and Drill in Human History*. London, 1995.
Miller, Geoffrey. *The Mating Mind*. London, 2000.
Mithen, Steven. *The Singing Neanderthals: The Origins of Music, Language, Mind, and Body*. Cambridge, MA: 2006.
Morley, Ian. "Evolution of the Physiological and Neurological Capacities for Music." *Cambridge Archaeological Journal* 12 (2002): 195–216.
Morris, Desmond. *The Naked Ape*. New York, 1967.
Morris, Desmond. "Typical Intensity and Its Relationship to the Problems of Ritualization." *Behaviour* 11 (1956): 1–12.
Okamoto, Hidehiko et al. "Listening to Tailor-Made Notched Music Reduces Tinnitus Loudness and Tinnitus-Related Auditory Cortex Activity." *Proceedings of the National Academy of Sciences* (2009). Online: http://www.pnas.org/cgi/doi/10.1073/pnas.0911268107 (accessed September 16, 2013).
Ovid. *Metamorphoses*. Translation by Sir Samuel Garth, John Dryden, et al. (1717). http://classics.mit.edu/Ovid/metam.html (accessed October 30, 2013).
Pahlen, Kurt. *Die große Geschichte der Musik*. Berlin, 2002.
Panksepp, Jaak, Günther Bernatzky. "Emotional Sounds and the Brain: The Neuro-affective Foundations of Musical Appreciation." *Behavioural Processes* 60 (2002): 133–55.
Papoušek, Mechthild. *Vom ersten Schrei zum ersten Wort. Anfänge der Sprachentwicklung in der vorsprachlichen Kommunikation*. Bern, 1994.
Patel, Aniruddh D. "Musical Rhythm, Linguistic Rhythm, and Human Evolution." *Music Perception* 24 (2006): 99–104.
Pinker, Steven. *The Language Instinct*. New York, 1994.
―――. *How the Mind Works*. New York, 1997.
―――. *The Blank Slate. The Modern Denial of Human Nature*. New York, 2002.
Plato. *The Republic*. Plato in Twelve Volumes, Vols. 5 and 6, translated by Paul Shorey. (Cambridge, MA; London, 1969).
―――. *Protagoras*, translated by Benjamin Jowett. http://classics.mit.edu/Plato/protagoras.html (accessed October 27, 2013).
Quaas, Beate. "Mut zum eigenen Sound: Ein Modell für musikalische Arbeit im Kindergarten. *Kindergarten heute* 1 (2002).
Rasmussen, Knud. *Der Sängerkrieg. Eskimosagen aus Grönland* (1922). Repr. Berlin, 1991.
Rousseau, Jean-Jacques. "Essai sur l'origine des langues où il est parlé de la mélodie et de l'imitation musicale" (1762). Translated by Dorothea and Peter Gülke. Wilhelmshaven, 1984.
Sachs, Curt. *Geist und Werden der Musikinstrumente*. Berlin, 1929.
Salmen, Walter. *Musikgeschichte in Bildern Vol. IV, No. 3: Haus- und Kammermusik*. Leipzig, 1969.
Schiefenhövel, Wulf and Blumtritt, Jörg. "Kommunikation – eine Einführung". In *Brockhaus Mensch, Natur, Technik: Phänomen Mensch*. Leipzig, 1999.

Schönberg, Arnold. *Harmonielehre*. Vienna, 1922.
Segler, Helmut. "Macht Singen dumm?" *Westermanns Pädagogische Beiträge* 3 (1976).
Standley, Jayne. "A Meta-analysis of the Efficacy of Music Therapy for Premature Infants." *Journal of Pediatric Nursing* 17, no. 2 (2002): 107–13.
Storr, Anthony. *Music and the Mind*. London, 1992.
Strauss, Richard. *Betrachtungen und Erinnerungen*. Zurich, 1949.
Stumpf, Carl. *Tonpsychologie* Vol. I/II. Leipzig, 1883/1890.
Stumpf, Carl. *Die Anfänge der Musik*. Leipzig, 1911.
Suppan, Wolfgang. *Der musizierende Mensch*. Mainz, 1984.
Tacitus. *Germania*. Translated and edited by Manfred Fuhrmann. Stuttgart, 1972.
Theodor W. Adorno. "Kritik des Musikanten." In *Dissonanzen*. Göttingen, 1956.
Timmermann, Tonius. "Rezeptive und aktive Musiktherapie in der Praxis" in *Die Heilkraft der Musik. Einführung in die Musiktherapie*, edited by Werner Kraus. Munich, 1998.
Trehub, Sandra et al. "Mothers and Fathers Singing to Infants." *Developmental Psychology* 33 (1997): 500–507.
Trehub, Sandra and Laurel Trainor. "Singing to Infants: Lullabies and Play-Songs." In *Advances in Infancy Research*, edited by Carolyn Rovee-Collier and Lewis P. Lipsitt, 43–77. Norwood, NJ, 1998.
Unbehaun, Jochen. *Musikunterricht. Alternative Modelle*. Bensheim, 1980.
Vaneechoutte, Mario and John Skoyles. "The Memetic Origin of Language: Modern Humans as Musical Primates." *Journal of Memetics: Evolutionary Models of Information Transmission* 2 (1998).
Wachsmann, Klaus. *Essays on Music and History in Africa*. Evanston, IL, 1971.
Wallin, Nils, Björn Merker and Steven Brown, eds. *The Origins of Music*. Cambridge, MA: 2000.
Wegner, Max. *Musikgeschichte in Bildern. Vol. II: Musik des Altertums / Lieferung 4: Griechenland)*, edited by Heinrich Besseler and Marius Schneider. Leipzig, 1963.
Zahavi, Amotz and Avishag Zahavi. *The Handicap Principle: A Missing Piece of Darwin's Puzzle*. Oxford, 1997.
Zatorre, Robert J. and Isabelle Peretz. *The Biological Foundations of Music*. New York, 2001.
Zentner, Marcel and Jerome Kagan. "Infants Perception of Consonance and Dissonance in Music." *Infant Behavior and Development* 21 (1998): 483–92.
Zimmer, Dieter E. *Tiefenschwindel. Die endlose und die beendbare Psychoanalyse*. Reinbek, 1986.

ACKNOWLEDGEMENTS

I would like to thank everyone who indirectly contributed to the creation of this book; the input that they have impressed upon me has been invaluable. Therefore, my thanks go to my human ethology teachers, Wulf Schiefenhövel and Irenäus Eibl-Eibesfeldt, as well as to the many people from whom I have learned a lot about music since my childhood – in the classroom, by making music together, in conversations or through their musical presence. I would like to mention by name Anita Arnusch, who evoked the initial spark in me as my first flute teacher; composer Peter Igelhoff, who was a family friend and musically present throughout my childhood; Herbert Feldmann, the singing principal of the elementary school at Ostpreußenstraße; Peter Chloé and Sebastian Reutter, two compelling music teachers and school musical directors; Bernd Edelmann, from the encyclopedic musicology faculty at the University of Munich; Max Frey, to whom I owe the most beautiful choir experiences; Barbara Schlick and Stephen Varcoe, who conveyed in their master classes what vocal devotion and rhetoric mean; the passionate conductor personalities of Enoch zu Guttenberg and Morten Schuldt-Jensen; and, finally, Dietrich Fischer-Dieskau, who provided his insights into the history of singing during a long conversation.